HORST HEGEWALD-KAWICH

My
Puppy

BARRON'S

TABLE OF CONTENTS

1   Typical Dog

2   How Dogs Like to Live

5 Grooming and Health Care

6 Training and Activities

How Dogs Talk

7

What to Do When There Are Problems

8

Appendix

Typical
Dog

Dogs are often our most loyal and dependable friends. They give us their devotion and never criticize us. All they ask in return is that we learn to understand canine nature.

What All Dogs Have in Common

Even if the behavior of our four-legged friends has been changed by thousands of years of living with humans, much of their wolfish heritage remains...

Recent genetic research using DNA analysis has scientifically proven that the dog (*Canis familiaris*) is descended from the wolf (*Canis lupus*).

Many thousands of years ago, when humans were still hunters and gatherers, they began domesticating the wolf. They probably started by raising wolf pups, and over the millennia, their efforts led to the development of the dog. Early humans didn't simply tame wolves; they actually "created" the dog by selectively breeding wolves raised in isolation. It's likely that this first came about for purely social reasons, because these early "wolf-dogs" had no practical use.

The women and children among our ancestors were doubtless just as delighted by their wolf pups as we are by our adorable puppies today.

In order to raise wolf pups, you need milk. However, at that time animals such as cows or goats had not yet been domesticated. Most likely it was the women themselves who provided milk for the pups, in addition to nursing their own children.

Imprinted on Humans

When the wolf pups were reared apart from their pack, they continued to develop strong social bonds through imprinting, but now they were imprinting on humans rather than wolves: Their wild relatives had become strangers to them. To this day, the dog holds a special place among domestic animals. No other species concentrates so exclusively on humans in its social relationships, and no animal bonds as closely with us or shows us as much devotion. That's why we find the dog such a lovable partner.

Wolf pups at play ▶
are just as frisky
as our puppies.

The First Year of Life

Dogs are highly intelligent, sensitive, and adaptable creatures with social behaviors that are very similar to our own.

The mechanisms of this innate social behavior must be trained and reinforced (imprinted), though, particularly during the first 16 weeks of the puppy's life. That's why it is so important to give the puppy regular opportunities to meet other dogs, both of the same age and older, as well as unfamiliar people, and to expose him to a wide variety of environmental stimuli. This actually lays the foundations for his later social behavior. The most important time in a dog's life is his first year. This period shapes the development of the dog's temperament and the character that results from his innate talents, and reflects the environment that we have fashioned for him.

Before the puppy reaches sexual maturity, he passes through the following developmental stages:

▸ Neonatal stage (weeks 1 and 2)
▸ Transitional stage (week 3)
▸ Imprinting stage (weeks 4 to 7)
▸ Socialization stage (weeks 8 to 12)
▸ Ranking stage (weeks 13 to 16)
▸ Pack organization stage (months 5 and 6), and finally
▸ Adolescent stage.

1 **"Family ties":** Puppies develop a strong feeling of belonging by playing together, even though things sometimes get a bit rough.

2 **Training for life:** Social roles and assertiveness are tested in mock battles, in which puppies practice behaviors necessary for survival.

The puppy on top is clearly demonstrating dominance and assertive behavior. ▶

Everything that the dog experiences during these developmental stages, whether positive or negative, seems as if it was inborn. In the learning process during the first year of life, the puppy's innate and acquired (including learned) behaviors merge and then appear as good, balanced temperament or poor, weak temperament. Whatever the dog misses now can never be made up later on.

The Dog's Temperament

"The dog's temperament is the sum of his innate and acquired behaviors as well as the internal state with which he responds to his environment." This statement embraces the bond with his human family, his behavior toward unfamiliar people and dogs, and his tendency to dominance. His temperament and vitality, his ability to learn, and his motivational readiness also play an important role.

Added to this are his instinctive intelligence (breed-specific, innate talents such as herding in Border Collies), working intelligence (revealed by how the dog performs at work or in sports), and adaptive intelligence (which the dog uses to take what he has learned, for instance as a police dog or hunting dog, and apply it correctly in a wide variety of situations to reach a desired goal). The dog's social intelligence determines his relationship with people.

What Wolves and Dogs Still Have in Common

Although most of our dog breeds no longer bear much resemblance to wolves in outward appearance, their kinship can still be seen in various physical attributes, in the senses and instincts they have inherited, and in their organs. In addition, more than a little canine behavior can be traced to the behavior of wolves and explained as perfectly natural, even though we occasionally find some of it undesirable. Despite these shared traits, though, we must realize that, as a result of domestication and environmental influences, our dog has long since ceased to be a wolf.

Physical similarities: Dogs are fleet-footed, and sometimes it is difficult to identify their gait at first glance. They can also change gaits in a flash, and they are skillful coursers, jumpers, and sometimes even climbers. Their skeleton (321 bones) is flexible because the bones are connected by joints, muscles, and tendons. Dogs walk on four toes. The fifth toe, the

In an underbite, the lower incisors protrude beyond the upper incisors, whereas in an overbite the lower incisors are located well to the rear of the upper ones and sometimes even touch the gums.

An adult dog has 42 permanent teeth, whereas a puppy has only 28 deciduous (baby) teeth. Puppies lose their baby teeth when they are four to six months old.

The internal organs: Like the dog's teeth, his digestive organs are those of a

DID YOU KNOW THAT...

...400 million dogs live on the street?

There are approximately 600 million dogs worldwide, of which about 400 million are strays, living on the street under the most miserable conditions. There are about 77 million pet dogs in the United States, but of these about 5 million wind up in animal shelters each year. Truly a sad fate for man's best friend.

dewclaw, is higher up on the inside of the foot. The dewclaw of the hind foot serves no useful function and is removed immediately after birth by sensible breeders because of the risk of injury it poses.

The dog's teeth naturally close in a scissors bite, in which the teeth of the upper jaw (except for the molars) overlap the lower row of teeth.

In some breeds, selective breeding has produced an underbite or overbite.

carnivore. The stomach is considerably larger than that of an herbivore. The digestive tract, on the other hand, is very short. To the dismay of many dog owners, our four-legged friend is also a scavenger. The heart of a healthy dog is designed for endurance, but it cannot recover as quickly after exertion as the wolf's. The lungs are also very efficient, as befits a coursing predator.

Scientific evidence clearly proves that the dog **is descended from the wolf.** Every dog owner should be aware of this.

Skin and hair: The dog's coat helps him control his body temperature by insulating him from heat and cold. Because his skin has no sweat glands or pores, he must cool off by panting. Among the wide variety of hair types that breeders have developed, the so-called double coat (consisting of a coarse outercoat and dense undercoat), seen in German Shepherd Dogs, most nearly resembles the wolf's coat and is best suited for all types of climates.

Extraordinary Senses

Of all the senses, only the ability to taste is more highly developed in humans than in dogs; otherwise we fall far short in any comparison. Our superior sense of taste is easy to explain, because the digestive system in dogs and wolves is geared to a natural diet: You won't find rabbit in tarragon sauce or duck á l'orange on nature's menu! On the other hand, scientific studies have shown that some dogs have almost telepathic abilities. For example, they alert their owners to an oncoming epileptic attack or a drop in blood sugar, or they warn of an impending earthquake days in advance. Likewise, their sense of direction and their ability to perceive the psychological state of their human companions never cease to amaze us.

Smell: Scents are composed of extremely tiny molecules that float in the air or adhere to objects. Dogs rely on specialized cells to detect these scents. A keen sniffer like the German Shepherd Dog, for example, has 220 million olfactory cells; a Dachshund, in comparison, has "only" 125 million, and a human has a measly 5 million. Through selective breeding, we have even improved on this superb innate ability, as for example in hunting and tracking dogs.

The sense of smell also plays an important role in the way dogs communicate with each other (olfactory communication). Whereas we perceive the world visually, the dog experiences his environment as intense olfactory images, which he stores in his memory.

"Muzzle licking" is an affectionate greeting ritual.
▼

Curiosity and a desire to explore are the motivating forces behind learning. Observing and sniffing everything in the environment fosters independence.

This olfactory memory helps him find his way perfectly time after time, and thanks to his excellent sense of smell, his homing ability frequently borders on the miraculous. That's why it is very important to encourage and develop this olfactory talent every day, even for puppies (see page 105).

Vision: Like their wolf ancestors, modern dogs still have an excellent ability to see movement, even though they no longer depend on this skill. They do not need to hunt in order to survive. Nevertheless, they can spot tiny, scurrying animals or moving vehicles even at great distances. Usually the stimulus of movement immediately triggers the dog's predatory instinct or pursuit drive (see page 129). Naturally, this can lead to dangerous situations in high-traffic areas if an untrained dog is not leashed.

Dogs do not perceive colors as well as people because, for predators, the color of the prey is not important. On the other hand, a reflective layer in the eye ensures that the dog's night vision is as good as that of the wolf. Dogs see colors in the yellow and blue parts of the spectrum; objects that we perceive as green are grayish to them, and red objects appear yellow.

Hearing: The natural ear shape is the erect "pricked" ear inherited from the wolf. The ears can swivel independently of each other, like radar dish antennas, and can locate and identify sounds coming from any direction. The dog can even hear frequencies in the ultrasound range (more than 20,000 Hertz), such as the pitter-patter of little mouse feet. His ability to detect very faint sounds is far superior to ours. Dog breeders have developed other ear types, though, such as the "semi-pricked ear" in Collies and the pendulous "drop ear" in many hunting breeds.

The practice of cutting or trimming the ears ("cropping") and tail ("docking"), common with breeds such as Boxers, is believed by some to affect the dogs' ability to communicate—not only with other dogs but with their owners as well—and is banned in some countries.

Touch: The dog's tactile sense allows him to perceive touch, temperature, and pain. The dog has tactile hairs (whiskers) equipped with extremely sensitive nerve endings on the cheeks, the chin, the eyebrows, and the "moustache." The skin of the nose ("nose leather"), the lips, the tongue, and the paw pads are especially sensitive. The sense of touch is very important in licking, pawing, and playing with other dogs. Even as a puppy, the dog learns to tell when his playmate feels pain and then in the future restrains himself when playing and roughhousing.

Those Wonderful Instincts

Everything that your dog does all day long is triggered and regulated by his instinctive drives.

How is Your Puppy's Temperament Developing?

Evaluate the development of your puppy's temperament in various situations. Record your findings. Regularly note positive or negative changes and try to find the reasons for them.

The test begins:
- How strong or weak is the puppy's bond with individual family members?
- How does he behave toward strangers, both human and canine?
- Does he submit willingly?
- How good are his temperament and vitality?
- How do you motivate him to play?

My test results:

Mothers and their offspring don't always want the same things. That's obviously the case here.

The following are the dog's most important instinctive drives:
▶ The pack instinct, important for subordination and obedience.
▶ The predatory instinct, necessary for hunting.
▶ The feeding instinct, essential for survival.
▶ The inquisitive instinct, the motivating force behind learning.
▶ The aggressive instinct, apparent in guarding and defending; it is not desirable in a family dog and should therefore be suppressed when you begin training your puppy.
▶ The flight instinct, which can save the dog's life.
▶ The sexual instinct, essential for preservation the species.
▶ The sleep instinct, which reduces stress.
▶ The grooming instinct, necessary

to maintain health; it includes comfort behaviors like stretching or shaking.
▶ The maternal instinct and nurturing instinct, needed by female dogs to raise puppies.
▶ The eliminative instinct, which must be regulated when housetraining a dog.

All these instinctive drives are inherited from the wolf; for the most part, they are still necessary for your dog's survival, even today, and can be triggered at any time by the appropriate stimulus. Through training you can simply inhibit these instincts or, if they are desirable, encourage them. You cannot, however, switch them off. Some instincts, like the sex drive, don't develop until the dog is mature. Others, such as the predatory instinct, are already fully developed in puppyhood but reveal themselves only through their specific outcomes (gratification of an instinct).

As an example, the predatory instinct is triggered by a "key stimulus" (for instance, a rabbit) and leads to a "drive state." This results in the corresponding "instinctual behavior" (in this case, hunting) with a possible "consummatory act" and "instinctual gratification" (seizing and killing the prey).

How quickly a dog responds to a stimulus depends on his stimulus threshold at the moment. With a low threshold, dogs react literally at the drop of a pin; with a higher threshold, on the other hand, it is difficult to "stimulate" the dog. In any particular dog, the level of the threshold is not only dependent on his personality, but can change from one occasion to the next. You'll learn more about canine instincts in later chapters.

An Introduction to Dog Breeds

Have you already fallen in love with a sweet little puppy of a particular breed? In this section, you'll find out what your pet will look like as a full-grown dog and what traits are characteristic of the breed.

As humans came to realize that dogs could be used for specific purposes, they deliberately set about mating only those animals that best met their requirements. The qualities they prized most highly were strength, speed, endurance, and health. At the same time, dogs living with humans began showing ever more diversity in size and shape; this was in part because of the intraspecific variability inherited from the wolf, but also because our ancestors reared some pups that were larger or smaller than normal or had unusual coat colors. Without human intervention, these dogs would not have survived in the wild. Breeds as such did not yet exist back then. Instead, these were hybrids of different canine varieties that would be described today as mixed breeds.

Selective Breeding

Purebred dogs first appeared in the middle of the 19th century—or, for some newer breeds, the beginning of the 20th century—when people started mating dogs of the same breed or same variety that had documented ancestries. Breeders began to keep studbooks and family trees (pedigrees) for this purpose. Since then, established breed standards prescribe the appearance of each breed. Even in the second half of the 19th century, though, people recognized the negative effect of inbreeding on this modern breeding practice. They discovered that mixed-breed dogs were usually unaffected by breed-specific hereditary diseases, because of a phenomenon known as hybrid vigor, or *heterosis*.

However, because breeders today try to achieve aesthetic goals and meet various breed standards that, in my opinion, are not always in the best interest of the animal, they no longer want to return to crossbreeding. In the breeding of domestic animals, however, it is employed purposefully and with great success to increase vitality.

TIP

Clubs and Organizations

Dog registries in North America include the American Kennel Club (AKC), American Rare Breed Association (ARBA), Canadian Kennel Club (CKC), North American Mixed Breed Registry (NAMBR), and United Kennel Club (UKC). The Kennel Club (KC) is the largest registry in Great Britain. The World Canine Organization (*Fédération Cynologique Internationale, FCI*), founded in 1911, is an umbrella organization with member clubs in many countries. (See Addresses, page 141.)

Breed Portraits
at a Glance

◀ West Highland White Terrier

The forebears of the "Westie" were brown Cairn Terriers. The white variety, the West Highland White Terrier, was developed so that hunters could tell it apart from rabbits and foxes. Today the Westie is one of the favorite breeds for households and families. He is often stubborn, but he makes up for it with his exceptional charm. In contrast to other terriers, he is not very aggressive.

Cavalier King Charles Spaniel ▶

In recent years, this beautiful dog has won a growing number of admirers. He meets all the requirements for a family dog, too, and is especially suited for city life. The Cavalier King Charles Spaniel loves to play with children and is easy to train.

Pug

He's a real character, and his fan club keeps getting bigger. Make sure that he has a well-developed nose.

Dachshund

He looks so innocent, but he's a crafty one. From a very young age, the Dachshund must be given consistent training; otherwise he will become top dog in the "dog-human pack." He can sometimes be a bit rough with children.

Miniature Schnauzer

This little fellow is every bit as clever as the Dachshund. The Miniature Schnauzer is a courageous adventurer and a good watchdog, although at times he can be quite vociferous.

Chihuahua

Although he's the smallest dog in the world, you still have to take the Chihuahua seriously. He is easy to train and alert.

West Highland White Terrier

According to breed lore, the Westie was developed from reddish brown Cairn Terriers after a hunting accident in which the favorite dog of the Malcolms of Poltalloch, Scotland, was mistaken for a fox and shot. It was easier to tell that the snow-white Westie was a dog. Starting in the 1970s, this dog became so fashionable that unscrupulous "puppy mills" made a fortune from it at the expense of breed quality. If you decide to buy a Westie, make sure you look for a reputable breeder. This small, self-confident dog is always ready for fun and has a great personality. Grooming requires some effort, though, because the coat must be trimmed regularly. An ideal dog for families and children, the Westie is also suitable for beginners and older adults.

Cavalier King Charles Spaniel

These dogs were favorites of English royalty. They resemble the King Charles Spaniel, but they are a bit smaller and have a somewhat shorter muzzle. The Cavalier King Charles Spaniel is an ideal dog for the city and has enjoyed a rapid increase in popularity in recent years. That led to large-scale production with intensive inbreeding, which resulted in a rise in the incidence of potentially fatal heart disease. When you get a puppy, check the medical history going back several generations. A cheerful, friendly, affectionate dog who is fond of people, the Cavalier loves walks but is just as happy to stay home when the weather is bad. Suitable for older adults and first-time dog owners.

Dachshund

Often kept as a hunting dog even today, the Dachshund was used in the Middle Ages to hunt badgers (the German name means "badger dog"). Today's purebred Dachshund dates from the late 1800s, when standards for the breed were developed. There are three different coat types (smooth, longhaired, and wirehaired). The American Kennel Club recognizes two sizes (Standard and Miniature), whereas the World Canine Organization (FCI) recognizes a third, smaller size (Rabbit Dachshund). Interestingly, under FCI rules the size is not measured by height at the shoulders, as in all other breeds, but rather by chest circumference. The Dachshund is very alert, affectionate, and clever. Be consistent with this dog, otherwise he will take over.

Pug

In the 17th century, the Pug arrived in Europe from China. His ancestors, supposedly bred from mastiffs more than 2,400 years ago, were once the companions of Buddhist monks. When brought to Holland by the Dutch East India Company, the Pug was first kept by aristocrats and kings. However, he has long been an ideal pet, puffing and panting happily through our homes. He is playful, friendly, and intelligent. The Pug is easy to train, but can sometimes be a bit stubborn. Buy only from breeders who have selected for a larger nose so that he can breathe more easily. An ideal companion for older dog lovers and beginners.

Chihuahua

The smallest dog in the world, the Chihuahua is thought to have lived among the Aztecs, although only as the shorthaired variety. Details about the origin of the breed remain uncertain. Some think that small dogs arrived in America with the Spanish conquerors in 1519. The Aztecs supposedly considered blue-coated animals sacred and sacrificed those with red coats on funeral pyres. The Chihuahua is affectionate, cuddly, easy to train, and alert. In encounters with large dogs, he sometimes succumbs to delusions of grandeur and ignores all the rules of dog behavior if not sufficiently socialized during the imprinting stage. He is not fond of wet or cold weather, and rambunctious children quickly get on his nerves. Well suited for older adults and first-time dog owners.

Miniature Schnauzer

The Miniature Schnauzer, a smaller version of the larger Schnauzers, was first recognized as a separate breed in 1899. Once an excellent ratter, he is kept today as a beloved canine companion. Unfortunately, indiscriminate breeding has introduced some temperament flaws and hereditary diseases. If the dog comes from good stock, he is a self-confident companion and a courageous but vociferous watchdog. He gets along well with children and other dogs and readily adapts to family life. Schnauzers generally shed very little but require regular coat care (trimming). If trained with consistency, he is an ideal companion, even for older adults and first-time dog owners.

Australian Shepherd

In the United States, the Australian Shepherd ranks among the "Top 30" favorite breeds. This lively dog needs lots of activity and challenging tasks to perform.

Poodle

The Poodle was originally bred as a water retriever. Many hunting and herding breeds have been developed from him.

American Cocker Spaniel

No wonder the beautiful Cocker Spaniel was once so popular. As a result, the dog suffered from indiscriminate breeding. Fortunately, though, responsible breeders are working to improve the quality of the breed today.

English Cocker Spaniel

Here is a black variety of the Cocker. The American Cocker Spaniel is descended from the English Cocker.

Labrador Retriever

Affectionately called the "Lab" by his fans, the Labrador Retriever is currently the number one dog for families and children. The Labrador Retriever is even-tempered and eager to please his owners. It is especially important for this dog to be treated as one of the family.

Parson Russell Terrier

The Parson Russell is a dog for active owners who can give him plenty of exercise.

Golden Retriever

This dog has a nearly white coat. The Golden, like the Labrador Retriever, is a keen swimmer and loves to retrieve.

Australian Shepherd

Sheepherders who immigrated to the United States from different countries brought their sheepdogs along with them. They crossed them with herding dogs of dingo and collie ancestry that came here along with sheep imported from Australia. The result was the Australian Shepherd, now one of America's most popular breeds. In recent years, this talented canine athlete has also taken the European dog sports scene by storm. The Australian Shepherd is tireless and lively, likes people, and gets along well with other animals. He learns easily and eagerly, but demands suitable tasks to challenge him as well as lots of exercise. A wonderful family dog for active beginners.

Poodle

This is an ancient breed, and not much is known about its origins. What's certain is that it was an excellent hunting dog, especially for water work. Many hunting and herding dogs were developed from this breed. Sizes to choose from are the Standard Poodle, Medium Poodle (not universally recognized), Miniature Poodle, and Toy Poodle. Between 1950 and 1970 the Poodle was considered quite fashionable, and the breed suffered enormously from indiscriminate breeding. In the hands of good breeders, he is now making a recovery. The Poodle is quick to learn. He loves to run, is robust, and wants to be included in all your activities. Although he has to be trimmed regularly, he doesn't shed. Ideal for first-time dog owners.

Cocker Spaniel

This dog was used to hunt woodcocks in the 19th century. The name *Spaniel* refers to the breed's origin from Spanish hunting dogs. They could flush game, "give tongue" to a scent (bark when pursuing their quarry), retrieve, and point out downed game to the hunter. Today almost all Spaniels are kept only as companion dogs. The best-known Cocker Spaniel breeds are the English and its descendant, the American. As family dogs, both types of Cocker are lively, playful, friendly, and open. Cockers are easy to train if you are consistent but not harsh. This dog needs lots of activity and enjoys canine sports, provided you don't overdo it. A dog for athletic first-time dog owners.

Labrador Retriever

Coat colors for this breed are black, yellow, and chocolate. In addition to being a good hunting dog, the Lab excels at narcotics detection, among other tasks, but above all he is an excellent guide dog for the blind. The Labrador Retriever is affectionate, even-tempered, patient and playful with children, and does not kill game or wander off. He needs training that is consistent but not harsh. Labrador Retrievers have a tendency to gain weight from overeating, and obese dogs become slow and lethargic. In southern Newfoundland, where this breed originated, the Labrador Retriever was used for water work, which explains his fondness for swimming. He is a trouble-free companion, even for first-time dog owners.

Golden Retriever

Lord Tweedmouth was the developer of this breed. In 1868, he crossed a yellow Labrador, a Tweed Water Spaniel, an Irish Setter, and a sandy Bloodhound, the parent breeds of the "Golden." The Golden Retriever resembles the Labrador in temperament. He is an adaptable family dog, although not quite so versatile as the Lab. You could describe the Golden Retriever as a real "sweetheart." Like the Labrador, he is an enthusiastic swimmer and retriever who needs lots of activity and consistent training. Unfortunately, because of their popularity, Goldens have suffered from indiscriminate breeding. However, a dog from a reputable breeder is suitable for first-time owners.

Parson Russell Terrier

Once known as the Parson Jack Russell Terrier or Jack Russell Terrier, this breed's name was changed by the AKC to the Parson Russell Terrier in 1999. Until 1980, these hunting terriers were bred for performance, as intended by the breed's developer, Parson Jack Russell. Now they are bred according to recognized standards. The "Sporting Parson" from Devon, in western England, preferred wirehaired dogs that were long-legged enough to accompany hunters on horseback but small enough to drive foxes out of their dens. A smaller version with much shorter legs is not recognized by the AKC. These are extremely energetic dogs. Because of their independence and stubborn assertiveness, they are not ideal companion dogs. Not for first-time owners or older people who value peace and quiet.

Great Dane

For reasons of space alone, few people today are able to keep such a magnificent yet enormous dog.

Great Dane

Great Danes reach a height of at least 28 inches (70 cm) at the shoulder. They are good-natured, want to be treated as part of the family, and need lots of exercise. Not for "couch potatoes."

Rough Collie

As "Lassie," the Collie became famous worldwide. This clever herding dog needs plenty of activity. Because of the Collie's sensitive nature, having an understanding human family is especially important. Collies love sports such as agility and obedience.

Airedale Terrier

This high-spirited terrier is eager to learn and easy to train. He needs lots of exercise and appropriate activities. A dog for active owners.

German Shepherd Dog

These two puppies are certainly adorable, and the German Shepherd Dog is without a doubt one of the most popular breeds, but this is not a dog for beginners. It takes careful socialization and good training to turn him into Rin Tin Tin.

Boxer

He is a bundle of energy who definitely needs to be kept busy with activities like dog sports. This affectionate, playful, and child-friendly dog is suitable for even first-time dog owners.

Bernese Mountain Dog

Even as a puppy, the Bernese Mountain Dog radiates the authority of an adult. With affectionate socialization and training, he will become a wonderful family dog.

Great Dane

Early Germanic tribes hunted for wild boar with mastiff-like dogs. Later on, only the nobility enjoyed the privilege of going on wild boar hunts with entire packs of gigantic dogs like these. However, since Otto von Bismarck made the Great Dane Germany's national dog, it has been kept merely as an imposing companion dog. For centuries, this dog has been bred for gentleness. With consistent training the Great Dane is good-natured and affectionate with his human family, children included. Because the Great Dane loves being part of the family, you need lots of room to house him. Keeping this dog in a kennel would make him sick. A Great Dane from a reputable breeder is a marvelous dog for experienced owners.

Collie

Originally the Rough Collie was a robust Scottish sheepherding dog. The breed was developed in the cold northern region of Scotland, where as working dogs they had shorter legs and a shorter nose than the elegant breed we know today. In the middle of the 19th century, once breeders crossed the Collie with Setters and Borzois and turned him into a show dog, his popularity soared. Indiscriminate breeding almost destroyed the breed, but the situation has improved. The Collie is clever, family oriented, and easily trained, a good watchdog with a strong protective instinct. However, he needs activity, and his magnificent, long coat requires a lot of care. Suitable even for first-time dog owners.

German Shepherd Dog

One of the most versatile breeds, the German Shepherd Dog has been used, among other things, as a herding dog, guard dog, police dog, guide dog for the blind, assistance dog for people with disabilities, and avalanche dog. No technical device can replace the German Shepherd Dog as a soldier's helper, a narcotics- or bomb-detection dog, or a cadaver dog. With consistent training, he fits right in with the family and gets along splendidly with children who have been taught to be responsible. He needs owners who can give him plenty of physical and mental activity every day. Vigilance and protectiveness are inherent traits and do not need to be further developed by special training. Not suitable for novice dog owners.

Airedale Terrier

This breed was developed in Yorkshire, England, from Otterhounds, Bull Terriers, Gordon Setters, and Black and Tan Terriers. The first breeder, Wilfried Holmes, created a versatile, courageous, weather-resistant dog. In the last two world wars, the Airedale Terrier demonstrated his capabilities as an ambulance dog and messenger dog. He is high-spirited, easily trained, and vigilant, and makes a great watchdog. He needs consistent training as well as activities that challenge him mentally. The coat must be clipped or stripped regularly. Even when well up in years, he can be a regular clown and a delightful companion. A dog for moderately experienced owners with a sense of humor.

Bernese Mountain Dog

The Bernese is one of the most beautiful farm dogs, whose main occupation was herding livestock. His popularity is growing by leaps and bounds. The breed would have almost died out in the late 19th century had not a breeder by the name of Franz Schertenleib discovered a few remaining individuals in the region around Bern, Switzerland. In the 1930s the dog was bred to be larger, which led to problems with temperament in some lines. Today he is an ideal "nanny dog" for children, affectionate and reliable but mistrustful of strangers. He loves walks and being outdoors, although he is not especially enamored of sports and running. Consistent training is sufficient to make him a pleasant and obedient dog for home and farm.

Boxer

One of the Boxer's ancestors, the Bullenbeisser, was used in Germany and Holland for hunting stags and wild boar. The modern Boxer was developed by crossing the Brabanter Bullenbeisser with Bavarian and other non-German breeds. By the 1860s, these crosses had produced a useful police and guard dog. The Boxer is friendly and playful but will defend his human family in earnest should the need arise. His patience with children is boundless. You can read his mood from his face. The Boxer needs loving but consistent training and lots of activity. He is suitable even for novice dog owners.

ADDITIONAL POPULAR BREEDS:
AN OVERVIEW

	Characteristics	Exercise and Activity Requirements
Saint Bernard	Well-bred dogs are good-natured and loyal, patient with children, and have a satisfactory protective instinct.	Exercise need not be vigorous, but it should be regular.
Border Collie	This dog is a bundle of energy with extraordinary intelligence; he's biddable, submissive, and lovable.	Even regular participation in agility sports is not enough to satisfy this dog's intelligence and need to work.
Boston Terrier	He is easygoing, affectionate toward people, and self-confident.	Very quickly learns tricks of any sort.
Dalmatian	A striking, lovable, high-spirited companion.	A Dalmatian can run along happily with bicyclists or horseback riders for hours.
French Bulldog	He is biddable, affectionate, gentle, always cheerful, and undemanding.	This dog doesn't need long walks, but wants to be with you, whatever you're doing.
Yorkshire Terrier	Assertive, intelligent, an excellent companion and watchdog; socialization and training a must.	This energetic dog gets lots of exercise indoors, so a daily walk around the block suffices.
Beagle	Good-natured, independent, with an excellent nose and a tendency to roam; needs socialization and obedience training.	Daily walks and romps satisfy this dog's need for moderate exercise.
Bulldog	Calm, affectionate, with a gentle temperament and charming personality.	Daily walks around the block are enough for this sedentary breed.
Shih Tzu	Once the companion of royalty in Imperial China, this little lapdog is affectionate, playful, and intelligent.	This toy breed appreciates short walks and occasional outdoor romps.
Pomeranian	A cheerful, self-confident, intelligent dog with boundless affection for his humans.	He doesn't need any particular activities. He is simply there, on guard.

Grooming Requirements	Suitability
His long coat needs a lot of attention.	He wants to be near his human family. He would get sick if kept in a kennel.
His silky coat is easy to care for.	This magnificent dog belongs with shepherds.
He does not shed or have a doggy smell.	For people who want a real dog that is not too big.
Coat care is simple, but the hair gets stuck in fabrics.	He needs active owners who love being outdoors.
The coat requires little care. Bulldogs love brush massages.	Suitable for people of all ages.
The long, silky coat needs to be brushed and combed daily; the hair on the head is usually tied up with a bow.	The Yorkie gets along with most animals and older children; he is well-suited to apartment living.
The short, hard coat only needs to be brushed once or twice a week.	Outgoing and friendly, the beagle gets along well with children and is happiest with an active family in town or country.
Give the short, soft coat a quick brushing once a week; the wrinkles on the face need to be cleaned frequently.	A wonderful companion, the Bulldog is good with children and adapts well to apartment life.
The long, flowing double coat requires daily grooming; the hair on the head is often tied in a topknot.	Friendly and sociable, the Shih Tzu gets along well with everyone and is a good choice for apartment dwellers.
Long coat comes in many beautiful colors and requires a great deal of attention.	For people of any age, but they should live out in the country because this enthusiastic watchdog barks loudly.

How Dogs Like to Live

Dog and owner: Truly a dream team, if there's a feeling of mutual understanding. And it's really not hard to achieve such a wonderful state of harmony.

Basic Rights of the Family Dog

It takes more than just good intentions to do right by a dog. Before you even get your puppy, it's important to learn all you can about canine nature.

You can't do justice to a dog's needs until you know what they are. All too often, though, enthusiastic animal lovers underestimate the dog's demands and the effort it takes to meet them. Make sure, then, that you understand what's in store for you before you bring a dog into your home.

Preliminary Considerations

First of all, make absolutely sure that *all* the members of your family are in agreement about getting a dog. Is anyone allergic to dogs?

If you rent your home, you need the approval of your landlord to keep a dog; if you live in a condominium, you'll usually need the consent of the other owners.

It takes a lot of knowledge, time, and patience to own a dog without running into problems. Before buying a dog, you have to consider whether or not just you or your entire family can meet the needs of a particular breed, one you may have been attracted to initially because of its appearance.

Time: Think about how much time you'll need to take care of a dog, regardless of breed. A dog requires supervision, care, and training or appropriate activity throughout the day; just how much depends on the breed. Along with at least two walks a day (half an hour each), you'll have to plan on several hours a day for all of this. Don't imagine for a minute, though, that a smaller dog takes less effort. Whether large or small, every dog, in principle, needs the same amount of attention over and above her breed-specific demands.

For puppies, it's just the greatest thing in the world: a lively romp, preferably with you as a playmate. ▶

Money: The financial burden of owning a dog can be considerable: The average fee for a dog license is $15, but in some areas it can be higher. In addition, you have to take into account insurance, food, annual vaccinations, equipment, and unexpected veterinary bills if the dog gets sick or injured (see Did you know, page 37).

Vacation: Even if you don't travel abroad on your vacation, it's not always possible to take the dog along when you stay at a hotel. If you can—something you should always confirm before your departure—you often have to deal with restrictions. I don't recommend traveling by plane with a puppy. It's too stressful for the youngster, and both the effort and expense involved are substantial. If you leave the dog at home, you need to find someone reliable to take care of her while you're away or else pay to board her in a good kennel. Of course, you shouldn't do this with a puppy who hasn't lived with you for very long.

What You Should Offer Your Dog

If you're hoping to share your life with a good-natured dog, then you must offer her the following things in this order:
▶ Activities and exercise
▶ Consistency and discipline
▶ Love and attention
Activities and related or additional exercise in the form of games should be the most important thing the puppy does with her owner (see page 36 and following).

Consistency and discipline have to do with the rules and limits you set when training a dog.

Love and attention are very important for the dog, but that doesn't mean you should be trying to win the dog's affection by constantly petting and pampering her. Demonstrate your love by taking care of her properly and meeting her needs. She experiences our affectionate care as positive reinforcement for her accomplishments.

What the Family Dog Is Entitled To

Naturally, the dog has a right to a healthful diet, clean quarters, and proper care (see Chapters 4 and 5). She is also entitled to freedom from injury, and appropriate social contact.

◀ *This looks like a wonderful friendship. Both puppy and child must learn how to treat each other properly, though, which requires your guidance as parents.*

A good "pack leader": What the dog hopes for as human "pack members" are knowledgeable animal lovers who will give her protection and security by behaving consistently as leaders and thereby earn her recognition and "respect." Many dog owners, though, fail to be acknowledged as leaders by their four-legged friends because they anthropomorphize them and judge them by human standards (see page 96). They do not understand the nature and abilities of dogs and therefore cannot meet their needs. You have to see your dog as an independent creature with her own individual needs that deserve respect. If the puppy is anthropomorphized and trained in an inconsistent manner, then the stage is set for later conflicts. The dog has trouble figuring just where her human belongs in the social order. She can no longer distinguish any sort of hierarchy. Even as a puppy, she sees her human's lack of leadership revealed in the chaotic conditions of the human-dog pack. Now, because of her innate pack instinct, she is forced to take over gradually as leader of the human-dog pack, something she will accomplish by the time she reaches sexual maturity. The dog doesn't do this because she is ambitious, like some people, but rather because her inborn pack instinct compels her to assume leadership in order to ensure the survival of the pack. To her bewilderment, though, she is now punished by her human for behavior that, from her perspective as the current "top dog," is necessary and therefore completely natural.

TEST

Is a Dog Right for Me?

When you see an adorable puppy, you immediately want to own a dog yourself. Before you get a dog, though, think carefully about whether you can give her the care she needs.

	Yes	No
1. Are all family members in agreement about keeping a dog, and are you sure no one is allergic to them?	○	○
2. Do you have enough room for a dog, and will your landlord allow you to keep one?	○	○
3. Do you have the time and temperament to take a dog out for two or three fairly long walks every day in all kinds of weather?	○	○
4. Will an adult dog be left alone daily for no more than two or three hours at a time?	○	○
5. Do you have enough expertise and time to train a dog and engage in activities with her?	○	○
6. Is there someone you can rely on to care for your dog if you are sick or away on vacation?	○	○
7. Are you prepared to assume all costs, including large veterinary bills?	○	○
8. Will your circumstances permit you to take care of a dog for an expected 10 to 15 years?	○	○

ANSWERS: If you can answer all questions with "yes," then a dog is just the right pet for you. Your four-legged friend will have a good life with you, because you are ready to assume full responsibility for her needs. If you have answered "no" to even one question, you should think carefully about whether a dog is really right for you.

Her Fondest Dream: A Dog

My 10-year-old daughter, Melanie, would love to have a dog, but we are not thrilled with the idea. What are we letting ourselves in for if we get a dog, and what should we be aware of so that we don't make any mistakes when we choose one?

When children want a dog, they usually have definite ideas about all the things they could do with her. In their dreams, they see themselves playing with her, romping around, going for walks, or teaching her tricks. You, as parents, are apparently willing to get a dog "just for your daughter" although you and your husband don't seem especially interested in the idea. Consider, however, that as adults, you will bear full responsibility for the animal, her care, and her training. Obviously, your daughter should assume certain tasks in order to learn responsibility and develop a strong bond with her dog. Under no circumstances, however, should you give your daughter complete responsibility for everything, alone and without supervision. At 10 years of age, she would find this far too much to handle.

A preliminary test

Here's my advice: First try to find out whether your daughter's desire is just a passing fancy; also see how you would manage with a dog. You could borrow a dog from friends for a weekend, for example, and if that goes well, offer your services as dog sitters when your friends go on vacation. Or, the two of you could take shelter dogs for walks for a few weeks. If you and your daughter pass this "endurance test," and if all of you are looking forward to getting a dog, only one question remains: Which dog should it be?

The right dog

Your daughter is probably dreaming of a particular breed. In this case, you must first make sure that the characteristic behaviors of this breed also meet with your approval and, above all, that you can provide the kind of activity this type of dog needs. Because no one breed is *the* perfect dog for all families or children, you should ask the advice of a dog expert, someone who can help you find the right dog. Naturally, every animal lover adores puppies, but do you think you can raise a puppy to be a well-mannered family dog? On the other hand, maybe you have already made the acquaintance of a somewhat older dog in the animal shelter. In this case you get to see not just her adult appearance, but also what sort of temperament she has. Here, too, of course, the advice of an expert more than pays for itself.

That's because, unlike humans, a dog always acts in a consistent manner when she is the highest-ranking member of the pack. If, as "boss," she has to discipline a human, she may resort to using her teeth if her previous warning signals went unheeded. The human regards this as undesirable behavior and takes the "disturbed" dog to a therapist. Fortunately, our dogs are so adaptable that not every situation ends badly. However, when children are the ones to suffer, it's already one incident too many. Today a large number of misunderstood pets suffer in private because their owners treated them as people rather than dogs. For this reason the puppy's owners must be well informed about their dream dog's breed-specific requirements and be certain that they can meet these needs throughout the entire life of the dog. An owner must be able to take the puppy's innate, purely instinctive, and not always desirable behavior, shape it through consistent but loving and patient training, and turn it into positive behavior. The dog's subsequent temperament is decidedly influenced by the quality of the person closest to him.

Today, humane dog ownership is impossible without an understanding of modern behavioral research. Every dog owner has a duty to become acquainted with this subject. If the puppy is adopted by people who have mastered the rules of communication, she usually has no problem learning to trust, forming a strong bond, and fitting into the human family (see page 93 and following).

Tip: Physical punishment of the dog has no ability whatsoever to strengthen your position as "pack leader" (see page 122 and following).

These two Dachshunds snuggling together are the best of friends.

Many family dogs no longer have any real work. Nevertheless,
they still need physical and mental stimulation
to stay healthy and enjoy life.

Being around people: Domestic dogs are absolutely dependent on people. They love being part of the activities of their human family, both indoors and out. For centuries, dogs accompanied humans almost round the clock, hunting, herding, or participating in any of the other occupations for which they were bred. Today it's not just the companion dogs who spend most of their time in our homes sitting and waiting. Even service dogs and working breeds rarely do breed-specific work anymore; instead, they have been demoted to elegant companions and usually spend most of the day waiting for short, boring walks around the block, which more often than not means dragging their unimaginative owners along behind them.

Wicker baskets like this tempt any puppy to chew.

▼

Exercise and activity: Depending on their breed and innate abilities, dogs need to be physically challenged by suitable activities and related unstructured exercise. Most dog owners mistakenly believe that the only reason their dogs need a lot of exercise is that they are descended from predators who hunted their prey by chasing after it.

Although an owner may take the dog for a walk several times a day, the dog gets very little out of it, because most of the time, she is allowed out only on a leash and has no "job" to do. A walk where she could run free and explore the area together with her favorite person, find the tracks of wild animals or the scent marks of other dogs, piddle on trees, or dig for mice would really be fun for her. Naturally, this sort of freedom demands discipline and obedience as well as a strong bond with her human companion.

Some dog owners even try to satisfy their dog's supposedly enormous need to run by having the leashed dog trot along beside them on monotonous bicycle rides. At best, that turns the dog into an athlete, but she still misses out on meaningful activity. Our dogs do not suffer from lack of exercise, but rather from not having any real work to do.

Jobs intended to suit the temperament of the dog and provide satisfying activity should challenge and stimulate her physically as well as mentally (see Chapter 6).

Dogs have always had an instinctive need to keep busy and in so doing move around naturally in a variety of ways. Wolves and wild dogs are on the go for 10 to 12 hours at a time searching for food. When they are doing this, their movement is always purposeful and goal oriented. No dog

intellectual development. Right from the start, then, you should give your puppy little tasks that she can accomplish successfully and that will challenge her.

In addition, even as a puppy your dog needs regular opportunities for social contact with other dogs: special puppy and/or dog parties in dog schools or clubs, playdates in dog parks, or

DID YOU KNOW THAT...

...it costs a lot to own a dog?

Here's an example of how much it costs to own a dog, assuming an average life of expectancy of 12 years: At 33 cents a day, the cost of food alone amounts to about $1,440 in 12 years. The dog license fee, which is about $15 a year on average, comes to about $180. Annual health insurance costs about $225, for a total of about $2,700. The cost of veterinary care for minor problems and regular vaccinations without any major diseases is about $235 a year, or $2,820 over 12 years. Add on about $1,000 for club dues and training courses. For equipment such as leashes, collars, dog baskets, food bowls of the most basic design, and a variety of grooming tools, you can figure on about $55 per year for a total of $660. Over 12 years the total cost is about $8,800. That's quite a tidy sum.

walks or runs just for the exercise, unless she has developed a behavioral abnormality from being kept in a confined space or chained up (so-called "kennel rage").

Even your puppy needs to keep busy and thus learns through her experiences, which in turn fosters

walks with other dogs and their owners. In addition to reinforcing her social behavior by playing with other dogs, this gives her more opportunity for healthy, dog-friendly exercise than you could offer her in almost any other way.

Everything for Your Four-Legged Friend!

A cozy bed, the right dishes for food and water, a good set of grooming tools, toys to ward off boredom, and, naturally, a well-fitting collar with matching leash for trips outdoors are all part of the puppy's basic equipment.

When the puppy moves in as a new member of your family, everything should go as smoothly as possible. Make sure you get all the basics before she arrives. Do your shopping at a good pet supply store, where you can ask for advice and inspect the quality of the merchandise before you buy.

A Comfortable Bed

Pet stores carry a wide assortment of dog beds. There are dog blankets made of soft polyester that absorb moisture; these are intended primarily for the car, but they can also be used for larger dogs as pads to cover the cold floor. Naturally, fluffier dog pillows filled with polystyrene beads or foam are much more comfortable. Our pampered pooches—especially the puppies—always like things warm and cozy, which means the beds should be made from soft fabric. Wicker baskets or nest-style beds made of hard plastic need additional blankets or padding—without a little "redecorating," they are probably uncomfortable. Of course, traditional wicker baskets often make irritating noises when the dog moves around in them. Besides, the woven twigs tempt even full-grown dogs to chew on them. Nests with high sides must be chosen to fit the size of the dog. Fleecy, foam-filled beds in all sizes and a wide variety of styles are also available at affordable prices. Keep in mind, though, that your puppy won't be full grown until she is 8 to 12 months old, and by that time she'll need a bigger bed. If you buy her a large bed right away to save money, she might feel lost and uncomfortable in it at first. Besides, it would be a shame to have an expensive dog bed chewed up. Make do, for the time being, by giving the puppy a little crate or a sturdy box that opens in the front, and put a padded mat on the bottom.

TIP

Quality Costs a Bit More

When buying accessories for your dog, don't be penny-wise and pound-foolish. Good-quality equipment is usually expensive, but in return it's often safer and more durable. Collars, for example, should fasten securely, and leashes should have sturdy hooks. Good dog pillows will stand up to more than one washing.

Alternatively, you could use a versatile carrier (see page 43). Smaller dogs, especially those with short hair, love cave-like beds where they can snuggle in luxury (see photo, right).

The right place: Dogs, just like us, need a place where they can get away from it all—when they are tired of roughhousing with the children, for instance—or where they can eat in peace. Sleeping and eating areas are off limits for children until the dog recognizes that they outrank her. The sleeping area must be in a quiet, draft-free spot that still affords the dog a good view of the rest of the room. As a rule, dogs don't sleep very soundly during the day. They are aware of almost everything that's going on around them indoors. The bed should never be placed in the entry area of the house, where the dog could be stressed by visitors. The same applies to the eating area. Defending an eating area, even when the dish is empty, has led to painful experiences more than once. During the day, large dogs usually seek out strategically important spots in the house or apartment, or else they simply lie on the floor; only at night do they retire to their comfortable bed. Put down a doggy blanket on your pet's favorite daytime spot, though, especially if you have a stone floor. All dogs place high value on comfort and are constantly looking for ways to make improvements. They like elevated resting places. Almost any dog would find a spot on the couch desirable. If she tries to keep you away from it during the day, she evidently doesn't have a very high opinion of you. In this case you should take steps immediately to counteract her dominant behavior.

In good hands

▶ 1 **Carrier:** During puppy training, a sturdy box like this is worth its weight in gold. The puppy can be accommodated here safely. It is also perfect for transporting him.

▶ 2 **Cozy cave:** A cozy, warm "cave" is a popular bed for puppies and even adult dogs of small breeds. Make sure that the pillow inside can be removed and washed.

Every puppy needs a soft, cozy bed.

Food and Water Bowls

Food and water bowls come in a wide variety of styles. The cheapest are made of plastic and are not recommended because they are too light weight and can be shoved around the room by the dog as she eats. Ceramic bowls are the sturdiest, but they are heavy and therefore harder to clean. Individual stainless steel bowls must have a rubber ring on the bottom so that they don't slide around. I suggest you get a sturdy double feeder with two stainless steel bowls (dishwasher safe) that can be raised or lowered to suit the dog (see photo, page 68). Shallow food bowls are preferable to deep ones.

The right spot: Set up the puppy's dining area in a quiet spot in home; it must always be accessible to the dog.

Collar, Leash, and Dog Whistle

Collar: I recommend an adjustable collar made of soft material that can "grow" along with the dog for one to two months. It must be wide enough to cover at least two of the puppy's neck vertebrae. The dog's cervical spine is just as vulnerable as ours. If you can't put a stop to your puppy's habit of tugging at the leash, then you should get her used to a harness for health reasons. This way, you'll relieve the pressure on her larynx and spine.

Leash: The puppy's leash must be appropriate for the size and energy level of the dog and should be about 6 feet (2 m) long. It should be as thin as possible, but absolutely tear-proof. It should never mean added weight for the puppy to drag around. Leash training begins, by the way, when you bring the puppy home. In Chapter 6, I'll describe different leashes used for training.

Dog whistle: A dual-tone whistle can help you call the dog when she's some distance away. The dog won't just come when you whistle, though; first you have to train her to respond to the sound.

Grooming Tools

A comb suitable for the length of the coat, a flea comb, and a stiff-bristle brush should be part of the basic equipment for every dog, no matter what kind of coat she has. Certain coat types require special grooming tools, such as a stripping knife or electric clippers.

Equipment
at a Glance

Collar and leash ▶
Puppy's basic equipment includes a flat, adjustable collar made of leather or nylon as well as a thin, 30-foot (10-m) leash to keep your dog safe in open country and a 6-foot (2-m) leash for "walkies."

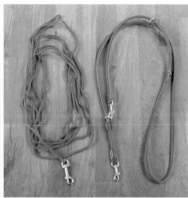

◀ Bed and bowls
A soft bed appropriate for the size of the dog is a must. It's also a good idea to get a sturdy elevated feeder; one with adjustable height is best (see photo, page 68).

Grooming and toys ▶
Important grooming tools: a brush (appropriate for the length of the puppy's coat), a comb, tick forceps, and tweezers. A small ball helps motivate your puppy to play.

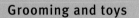

How Does Your Puppy Play?

Which games are good for motivating your dog, and what does she find less stimulating? Try playing different games and see how she responds. Does she like active games, is she subdued when she plays, or is she the nervous type?

The test begins:

○ The energetic type: She is easily excited, very active, and aggressive or dominant when playing.
○ The phlegmatic type: She plays quietly, steadily, sometimes awkwardly, and stops playing immediately when she is no longer motivated.
○ The nervous type: She is easily inhibited and influenced when she plays. She readily submits to a more dominant playmate.

My test results:

Either the breeder or the pet supply dealer can recommend a suitable comb or brush for your dog (see Chapter 5). It's also a good idea to get a special super-absorbent dog towel that you can use to clean off the dog, for instance after a walk in the rain.

Toys

Here are some of the most popular games and toys for you and your dog:

Fetching games: The best toy for a traditional game of fetch is a hard rubber ball that's the right size for the puppy; it is more durable and easier to clean than the usual rubber ball or tennis ball. Besides, modern tennis balls can damage the dog's teeth and may even be a health hazard because they are waterproofed to make them last longer. Of the various squeaky toys, the classic hedgehog balls are best for young puppies because they don't roll as fast as regular balls and they make prey-like squeaking sounds that help motivate the puppy. With other squeaky toys, make sure they are ball-like so that they encourage the dog to chase and catch them.

A Kong on a sturdy rope makes a great throw toy and belongs in every puppy's toy box.

Because of its unique shape, the Kong bounces erratically when it hits the ground, unlike a ball. It is more difficult to catch, and that makes it especially popular with dogs who love to fetch. A toy that floats in the water and a prey dummy that can be stuffed with food (see page 105) are perfect for training games.

Tug toys and chew toys: To challenge your puppy physically in a game of tug-of-war, start by giving her a soft towel as a prey substitute. Later on, you can use a small jute tug toy or one of the colorful rope toys sold at pet supply stores (see Chapter 6).

Toys for solitary play: The pet store carries a wide variety of toys that will keep the dog occupied when she is left alone.

The Crate

It's helpful to get a sturdy dog crate as a secure place to house your dog. You need to keep an eye on the puppy at all times, especially in the first few weeks, but if you can't watch her for a while because you're busy doing something else, then you'll have to confine her to the crate temporarily. Safe in her crate, she can't get into mischief elsewhere in the house or disturb you while you're working. The crate is also very practical for housetraining (see Chapter 3), and properly secured, it can be used in the car as a travel carrier.

For now, it only has to be large enough to allow the puppy to stand, sit, or stretch out comfortably when she lies down. Put her puppy blanket in the crate, the one whose scent is familiar from her old home and on which she has slept since being separated from her mother and littermates. A blanket draped over the crate turns it into a cozy cave perfect for sleeping. If you buy a crate large enough for her when she's full grown, you'll spare yourself the expense of buying a second crate later on. In the beginning, you can partition off part of the crate to make it puppy-sized.

A favorite toy always motivates the puppy to play. It's often treasured and doesn't get chewed up.

Welcome Home

It really doesn't matter how cute a puppy looks. What counts is whether he's right for you and your way of life. Take plenty of time choosing your "dream dog."

Best of Friends

If you use your head as well as your heart when choosing your "dream dog," chances are the two of you will enjoy a wonderful, long-term relationship. This means you have to prepare carefully.

Dog and human must be right for each other if their life together is to be harmonious. Although most dog lovers already have a "dream dog" in mind, the breed's requirements are not always compatible with their way of life. In this case, problems are often unavoidable.

Analyze Your Lifestyle

Take, for example, the Border Collie: This is a great dog and very intelligent, but he needs a lot of physical and mental activity. Someone who is older or not very active will certainly not be happy with him. On the other hand, an athletic young man with an English Bulldog—a dog who is content to live by Winston Churchill's motto of "No sports!"—would probably take little delight in his lazybones unless he loves the dog's other merits. To find a puppy that is right for you and your family and be able to give him the care he needs, you need to learn about the behavioral traits of different breeds.

To do this, it is helpful to study the breed groups of organizations like the American Kennel Club (which categorizes more than 150 breeds in

7 groups) or the World Canine Organization (more than 330 breeds in 10 groups).

If you are looking for a family dog or a dog for senior citizens, then you could find what you're looking for among the companion dog breeds. But if you want a larger family dog—and you have plenty of room—you should consider good-natured breeds such as Labrador Retrievers or Golden Retrievers, or perhaps more sedate dogs such as the even-tempered Newfoundland.

Who can resist such a captivating puppy? ▶

45

TEST

Submissive or Dominant?

Place the puppy on his back and put one hand on his chest to hold him still (see photos, pages 48 and 49). This way you can test his temperament. Incidentally, don't confuse submissive behavior with fearfulness. Submissiveness toward a higher-ranking individual is completely normal.

	Yes	No
1. The puppy does not resist, is relaxed, and may even lick your hand.	○	○
2. He struggles briefly but remains calm and relaxed.	○	○
3. The puppy is tense and keeps struggling and kicking.	○	○
4. The puppy struggles constantly, growls, and bites.	○	○
5. The puppy freezes and clamps his tail between his legs.	○	○

ASSESSMENT: Depending on how your "dream" puppy performed in this test and which questions you answered with a "yes," the temperament assessment is as follows:

1. A well-imprinted and well-socialized puppy; he is submissive.
2. A well-socialized puppy who submits with a little bit of pressure.
3. A moderately well-socialized puppy who reacts somewhat indifferently. Without proper training, he could develop into a dominant dog.
4. A dominant puppy who sets his own rules and is poorly socialized.
5. A timid puppy who is poorly socialized and is not well imprinted on people.

There are considerably more options for athletic and active people. They can choose from among the many working breeds, including hunting dogs, herding dogs, and terriers, all of which need lots of activity, exercise, consistent training, and conscientious care.

If you would like a mixed-breed puppy, then try to find out which breeds are part of his ancestry; that's the only way you can guess what your adorable "surprise package" has in store for you as far as appearance, size, and character are concerned. If you don't make any serious mistakes in raising him, then you probably won't have many problems with your dog.

A Puppy from a Breeder

If you have fallen in love with a particular breed, then you'll have to head for a breeder. Just make sure he or she is reputable. Unfortunately, some unethical breeders are in it only for the money, and these "black sheep" cause a lot of problems. The result is often sick dogs with congenital defects. They are sold over the Internet or in the newspaper at lower prices than dogs from reputable breeders; consequently, they manage to find naïve buyers who believe they have found a "bargain." The puppies are often shipped to buyers from out of state or handed over in private homes. The buyers never get to see the mother dogs or the breeding facilities.

They also have a very limited selection because they are led to believe that all the other puppies sold like "hotcakes" and this is the only one left. Frequently the dogs are less than eight weeks old and are so stressed that they get very sick in their new home because they are too young to have a well-developed immune system.

Sometimes it is not possible to vaccinate them properly. Severe temperament flaws and chronic diseases often don't appear until the dogs are older. Stay away from shady deals like this!

How to recognize a good breeder: He or she is usually a member of a breed club affiliated with one of the major kennel clubs and complies with their breed standards. The largest of these clubs in North America are the American Kennel Club, the United Kennel Club, and the Canadian Kennel Club. These national registries maintain studbooks for each breed, and they can trace a dog's ancestry back for many generations. If you are looking for a purebred puppy, the breed clubs and kennel clubs can also help you locate breeders in your area.

When choosing a puppy, you should get an idea of the breeding facilities by visiting them in person. Do the overall surroundings and the kennel seem clean and well tended? The breeder should have at most one or two breeding females and raise no more than two litters per year. The dogs live in the breeder's home, not exclusively in the kennels. Older females that are no longer used for breeding should be retired. As a rule you will not see the father of the puppies because the female is usually taken to the male's home to be bred. A good breeder will ask for details about how and where you live and may want to see you and your family several times before you adopt your puppy in order to get an idea of where the puppy will be living. The puppies should have frequent contact with strangers, especially children, before they are eight weeks old.

It's so hard to choose! Which puppy should it be? It's best if you ask the advice of a dog expert. ▶

The Puppy Test

▶ **1** **Dominant:** The puppy is held firmly but gently and prevented from moving. A dominant puppy growls and bites.

▶ **2** **Relaxed:** A well-imprinted and well-socialized puppy is very relaxed and does not struggle. However, this submissiveness is not a sign of fear.

▶ **3** **Carrying properly:** Place one hand under the puppy's chest and the other under his rear end. This way nothing can happen.

Many breeders have a little puppy playground in their yard with a variety of toys where the youngsters can start developing their body awareness, courage, and agility. Brief outings close to home with their mother or short rides in the car enrich the puppies' store of positive experiences.

Papers: The puppy should be at least eight weeks old when you adopt him, and he must be vaccinated, dewormed, and have a microchip or tattoo for identification. The breeder will let you see the pedigrees of the parents and the litter registration; he will give you the puppy's registration papers along with the sales contract, vaccination record, and deworming schedule.

A Puppy from a Private Seller

You may have an opportunity to get a puppy from a private household. These are usually mixed-breed pups, so naturally the owner can't provide a pedigree for them, but this doesn't necessarily mean they have problems right from the start. Nevertheless, the risk is quite high, because the puppy's parents have usually not been checked to see if they are suitable for breeding; more likely than not, they have become parents by accident. Animals like this are sometimes advertised in the newspaper or on the Internet as mixed-breed puppies "from a loving home." Be careful, though! Some sellers are crooks who play on your sympathy; they deliberately mate dogs to produce supposedly new breeds, which they then furnish with imaginative names in order to make a lot of money. Usually these cute dogs are crosses of miniature breeds, and unsuspecting buyers fall for them. Naturally, these dogs don't have papers.

If you are still interested in a puppy like this, ask the advice of an expert when you go to look at the puppies.

A Shelter Puppy

Sometimes you can get a puppy from an animal shelter. In this case, try to find out what the puppy has already experienced since birth. You must understand that you could get a puppy who might not have grown up under the best conditions and who may have been negatively imprinted during those important first weeks (see page 8). Yet with lots of understanding, love, and patience, a shelter puppy can certainly develop into a wonderful family dog. Don't ever decide to get a dog from a shelter just because it is cheaper; instead, realize that although you may have to overcome minor problems, you are offering an animal the chance for a happy life.

What to Look For

Mother dogs and pups should behave in an uninhibited and friendly way around you, and they should all look healthy and clean. Don't buy a puppy if you can't see the mother. The same holds true if you can't visit the puppies, or if the mother and/or the puppies seem afraid and hide.

TIP

How to Recognize a Healthy Puppy

He looks alert, watches what's going on around him, and is easy to motivate. He has a smooth, shiny coat and clear eyes without any discharge. Mouth, nose, eyes, ears, and anus are clean and pleasant smelling. He is active, his movements are coordinated, and he has a good appetite but is not too fat.

I also advise you against buying if the puppies are apathetic, cannot be motivated, and look sick (see Tip, page 49). If the puppies are covered with feces, smell like urine, and have potbellies, under no circumstances should you buy the poor creatures out of pity. Unfortunately, many people still do this, which only supports unscrupulous dog breeders.

If you have your pick of the litter, though, don't take the biggest or the smallest, nor the boldest or the shyest (see The Puppy Test, page 48).

If you don't trust yourself to choose the right puppy for you and your family, then ask the advice of someone who has a lot of experience with dogs. This wise decision can reward you and your four-legged friend with many happy years together.

DID YOU KNOW THAT...

...there are different systems for categorizing dog breeds?

There are more than 400 dog breeds in the world, and different kennel clubs group them in different ways. The World Canine Organization (FCI) recognizes 339 breeds, which it categorizes using the following system: Group 1: sheepdogs and cattle dogs (except Swiss cattle dogs); Group 2: pinschers and schnauzers, molossoid breeds, Swiss mountain and cattle dogs; Group 3: terriers; Group 4: dachshunds; Group 5: spitz and primitive types; Group 6: scenthounds and related breeds; Group 7: pointing dogs; Group 8: retrievers, flushing dogs, water dogs; Group 9: companion and toy dogs; Group 10: sighthounds. The American Kennel Club (AKC) recognizes more than 150 breeds and categorizes them as follows: Group I. sporting dogs; Group II. hounds; Group III. working dogs; Group IV. terriers; Group V. toys; Group VI. non-sporting dogs; Group VII: herding dogs.

A good breeder will help you choose the puppy that's best for you. A shy puppy would not be happy in a family with very active children, and a self-confident, headstrong, feisty puppy would soon have inconsistent owners wrapped around his little paw.

Male or Female?

In my experience, it is not important whether you get a male or a female as long as the dog receives consistent, loving training. How obedient ("tractable") a dog is depends on the individual.

There is not much difference in temperament **between males and females**. How obedient a dog is depends primarily on the owner.

The generalization that females are easier to socialize and take less time to train is not true, because this largely depends on the talent of the dog owner.

In most breeds, the males are larger, stronger, and generally appear more imposing. In their relationships with other dogs, males have more of a tendency to engage in posturing and dominance behaviors. Especially in service dogs and working breeds (for example, German Shepherd Dogs, Doberman Pinschers, Rottweilers) the males are often more self-confident than the females. Some dog owners insist that male dogs are ready to breed all year-round and are basically interested in all "lady dogs," unlike females who are in heat only for about three or four weeks twice a year. In my opinion, they are confusing dog behavior with the way many "lords of creation" treat women. As a rule, males are peaceable and easy going year-round. They are friendly and playful toward females who are not in heat. Only when a female broadcasts sexual signals in the form of strong scents does she awaken sexual interest in the male. It would be unnatural for a male to be interested in females all the time. If this happened in a pack of wolves or wild dogs or in a multiple-dog household, there would be a constant state of sexual tension; it would be impossible to keep the peace in a group like this. If you have an intact (unspayed) female, which is something I would strongly discourage, it is your duty to choose a route for your daily walks when she is in heat so that she doesn't drive all the neighborhood males into a state of sexual madness by leaving a trail of scented calling cards (see Spaying, page 90). When your female is in heat, she should not be allowed outdoors alone, because the neighbors' dogs are out there, and females in heat will go looking for a male on their own. All of the females I have owned over the past 40 years have been spayed; they were good-natured and did not suffer from sexual stress.

Puppy games: Here's a cheerful invitation to a little play-fighting.
▼

The Puppy's Arrival

Incredible but true. The first hours and days with your little four-legged friend in his new home shape your future life together. Take your time, then, and tackle everything together at a leisurely pace.

The big day is here at last. Today you are bringing your puppy home. You're prepared for his arrival, and everything he needs is ready (see page 38).

The Trip Home

Usually your new four-legged family member doesn't live nearby, but he's not terribly far away either, so you bring him home by car. To make sure the puppy has a gentle and relaxing trip, you need to keep a few things in mind:

▶ Even if you usually do the driving, content yourself with being a passenger for this trip so that you can devote your attention to your puppy.

▶ Plan the trip so that you arrive home before dark. Then your puppy will have enough time to explore his new surroundings.

▶ Don't give the puppy anything to eat for at least five hours before the trip; this way he won't get carsick during the ride.

▶ Don't make the dog stay by himself in a carrier or—if you have a station wagon—in the back of the car. If his memories of this first trip are tinged with fear, he won't want to ride in the car in the future.

▶ Sit in the backseat holding the puppy in your arms. On the seat next to you is a dog basket with a blanket that has the scent of his littermates and his mother. Put the puppy in this basket once he has fallen asleep in your arms.

▶ Have a cloth towel and a roll of paper towels handy in case there's an "accident."

▶ If the trip takes longer than an hour, stop for a break every hour unless he is asleep.

▶ During the breaks, put him on a leash and walk back and forth with him for a few minutes so he can go to the bathroom.

▶ If the dog starts to feel sick, you'll be able to tell by his panting and the watery discharge from his mouth. Get out of the car with him immediately and walk him around until he behaves normally again.

Arrival in the New Home

Once you get home, take the puppy outside right away to visit the spot where he should always do his "business" in the future. My trick: I get a little bit of dog poop from the breeder and put it in my new arrival's future toilet area. The familiar smell will motivate him to relieve himself there.

Dog pillows are stuffed with shredded foam or polyester fill. It makes a wonderfully soft bed for the puppy.

Give the puppy some water to drink, and stay outside with him at least until he has urinated. Only then should you bring him indoors.

Rest: The last thing the puppy needs just now is a reception committee of excited adults and lively children. What he requires most of all is rest, and he should get it over the next few days.

Exploring: First, let the puppy explore the house in peace and quiet. When he gets tired after a while, put him in his basket or in the carrier, which is already familiar from the trip home, and let him sleep. As soon as he wakes up, though, take him to his "toilet area." Wait there until he has relieved himself, praising him enthusiastically as he goes about his business. Now you can give him his first meal, which for the time being should be the food he is used to from the breeder or his "old" home. If

he hasn't had a bowel movement yet, you'll have to take him outside again after he eats.

Meeting the family: Children should not play with the puppy too much in the first few days. That would overtax him. Let the puppy approach other family members when he's ready. He needs a few days to get acquainted with "his" people and adjust to them.

Learn the daily routine: The next step: Where is the water, where can he eat, where does he sleep, and, above all, what's the daily routine in the new pack? The puppy must be able to figure all this out at his own pace.

Once the puppy gets to know all this, he will be able to cope with unfamiliar visitors and relatives. Make sure he can still get lots of sleep and that he isn't disturbed by anybody, especially the children. Otherwise you may wind up with a nervous dog with behavioral problems.

Let your puppy take **his time getting** acquainted with his surroundings.

Strengthen the relationship: In the first weeks, the puppy should bond only with his caregiver and immediate family members. That's why you shouldn't leave the dog in the care of strangers, even for a short time. It will be a few months before he knows where he belongs. Then maybe the neighbors

This is the way to find out just who has a better grip.

▼

can look after him for a couple of hours. That's also when other children or friends can come to play with the puppy, but only under your supervision.

The first nights: These are a key experience for the puppy; at the same time, they mean the beginning of nighttime housetraining. My experience: A "new arrival" sleeps with me in my bed for the first two or three nights. First of all, this helps him form a strong bond with me; secondly, it gives me better control of the "leaky" little fellow as far as housetraining is concerned, even at night. As soon as he stirs, I carry him out into the yard to his toilet area. If you don't want to make this extra effort in the beginning or are absolutely opposed to letting the dog sleep in your bed, it can often take months or even longer until the dog is housetrained. After a few days my puppy sleeps near my bed in a suitable basket or in a tub, but one he can't climb out of on his own. He indicates by his restlessness when he has to "go." As a matter of fact, dogs are inherently clean animals, and it goes against their nature to soil their sleeping area. It's just important that you wake up and notice when he has to go. The new bed should not be so big that the puppy can piddle in one part of the basket and go back to sleep in another part where it's still nice and dry (see page 38). Place the puppy's bed very close to yours so that he senses your presence. I've found that with consistent nighttime monitoring, a puppy will be sleeping through the night in 8 to 14 days. However, you have to take him outside immediately each time he wakes up.

Once your puppy has slept through the night for at least a week without "leaking" and you would like him to start sleeping in a different place in the bedroom or in another room, shift his bed a few feet every day until you get it to the desired spot. Move it only if he slept peacefully the night before, though.

Housetraining

In the first weeks, you have to keep an eye on the puppy constantly when he's indoors, regardless of what he's doing at the moment. Basically, the puppy is allowed to roam free in a room only where you can watch him as closely as you would a toddler. If, for some reason, that is temporarily impossible, then put him in his crate or carrier, where you've left one or two marvelous treats for him to find. He'll soon fall asleep, and you won't have to be checking on him constantly. You will hear when he wakes up again and wants out. There are certain times when you can expect that a puppy will have to relieve himself: right after he has eaten or had a drink, as soon as he wakes up, or after a prolonged stay in his crate or carrier. Then you'll have to get him outdoors as quickly as possible so that he can take care of "business." If the puppy suddenly stops playing and starts sniffing the floor intently, hunches his back and squats down, or turns around in a circle, you should pick him up with a loud "No!" and carry him outside as fast as you can, because this is how he gets ready to have a bowel movement.

CHECKLIST

Puppy-proofing

Imagine you have a toddler. That's exactly what it's like when the new member of your family is a puppy:

1. Put away any hazardous objects within reach of the puppy.

2. Secure any exposed electric cords.

3. Prevent access to stairways with infant gates (available in pet stores as "pet gates").

4. Store chemicals such as cleaners, fertilizers, snail bait or other pesticides, and medications in a safe place.

5. Make sure you don't leave any small items lying around where the puppy can get to them, for instance toys (Legos, marbles, beads, etc.), ping-pong balls, needles, or sharp objects.

6. Houseplants and garden plants that are poisonous for dogs include hellebore, yew, angel's trumpet, foxglove, laburnum, autumn crocus, hyacinth, boxwood, cherry laurel, arborvitae, lily-of-the-valley, mistletoe, nightshades (deadly nightshade), oleander, daffodils, spindle tree, rhododendron, delphinium, horse chestnut, poison hemlock, snowdrops, holly, and savin juniper (see Useful websites, page 141).

7. Fence off garden ponds and open cellarways. Also fence off flower beds and valuable young trees and shrubs so the puppy doesn't chew on them; no plant is safe from the sharp little teeth of an enterprising puppy.

8. Is the fence enclosing your yard really escape-proof?

9. If you have small pets such as guinea pigs, hamsters, or birds, place their cage where the puppy can't reach it (more to protect them than for the puppy's safety). This way he won't be tempted to pester the animals, and he can gradually get used to the other pets that share his home.

◀ *There are plenty of opportunities to carry a puppy when he is young, but by and large he should be allowed to use his own four legs.*

He may urinate faster, depending how urgent it is, and you might not be able to get to him on time. But if you catch him in the act, give him a stern "No!" while he's piddling and take him outside right away. If he "forgets" in your absence, then you have to ignore the accident. Hitting him or rubbing his nose in his "business" only destroys his trust in you. He will not make the connection between the "punishment" and his action. It's a good idea, then, to take the puppy outside briefly every half hour in the beginning, just to be on the safe side. This way, you'll soon become familiar with your dog's "bathroom rhythm" and will be able to adjust your timing accordingly.

What the Puppy Has to Learn

Name: It's easiest to pronounce two-syllable names that end with a vowel like *a*, *e*, or *u*. The name should fit the dog. If you say your puppy's name in a friendly tone of voice and, in the beginning, always accompany it with a treat or a caress, he will soon respond to it. On the other hand, if you have to call him back sternly to stop him from doing something inappropriate, then you shouldn't use his name together with an admonishing "No!" or "Yuck!" Otherwise, he will associate his name with something negative.

Wearing a collar: A good breeder gets the puppies used to wearing a collar before giving them away. In general, though, the puppy's first encounter with the irksome collar comes when he leaves for his new home. As you put it on him for the first time, give him a tasty snack; for the first few days, leave it on the dog except at night.

When you put it on again, give him another treat at the same time. After a few days he'll be used to the collar, and then you'll need to put it on only for walks and possibly for training.

The First Time Outside

Many first-time dog owners want to take their puppy for walks right away. Inexperienced puppies, in particular, refuse to go along because they are frightened; they panic and want to go back to the house. During the first two weeks, it is enough if the puppy gets to know his own yard or the toilet area on the grassy strip outside the apartment building. Only once he feels secure there will he show any interest in exploring the world beyond. You can't take a puppy for a brisk walk; instead, let his curiosity have free rein. He has to investigate everything for himself. Usually the puppy first gets to know his surroundings with you— the noise of the traffic, the smells of the street, the strange people, and, naturally, the unfamiliar dogs. A short trip "once around the block" is quite enough. And here's another tip: Before the next vaccination, you should take your puppy to the veterinarian for a social visit once or twice. He'll get a dog yummy from the veterinarian without having to be treated. By the next visit, he'll no longer be afraid.

MY PET

How Is Your Puppy Developing?

A "puppy diary" is valuable not just as a memento, but also as a way to keep track of your healthy puppy as he grows. That's why you should regularly record these rapid changes.

The test begins:
○ Every week take photos of your puppy standing, sitting, or in action.
○ Measure the puppy's height, length, chest circumference, and neck circumference weekly.
○ Weigh him once a week and compare his weight gain with the table on pages 71 and 72.
Enter all changes and unusual observations in the diary.

My test results:

Questions About
Acclimation

? Do you have any additional tips on how to prevent our puppy from having "accidents" at night?

Give him the last meal of the day, including water, before 6 P.M. Until about 10 P.M. the puppy should have an opportunity to go to the bathroom every hour. Take him outside one last time before you go to bed yourself. Let him have water again first thing in the morning.

? Will a puppy get along with other pets?

You may have problems getting him used to resident pets. Small animals like dwarf rabbits and hamsters are among the dog's natural prey. There is no guarantee that the dog will be able to control his prey drive indefinitely and at least tolerate these pets. Put the cage where the puppy can't reach it. This way he can get used to it slowly. On the other hand, living with a cat usually presents no

problems, and it's not uncommon for fast friendships to develop. Cats usually train the puppy themselves. Simply restrain the puppy during the first few days when he wants to chase the cat.

? Can I leave my 12-week-old puppy alone for a while in the house yet?

No, the puppy is still not housetrained. Besides, he first has to learn to stay by himself in another room. While you're working around the house, "accidentally" close the door behind you and ignore any protest he may make. Don't "free" him until he has been quiet for a little while. Then simply open the door, but don't pay any further attention to him. He must learn that he can trust you and that you will always come back. It also helps to have a crate (see page 43) where he can find something to chew while you run downstairs, for example. When you come back, you must not

pay any attention to the puppy or comfort him. Wait 10 minutes and then let him out of the crate without saying a word.

? I bought a portable carrier for our puppy for car trips. However, he absolutely refuses to go into it. What are we doing wrong?

For one day, give your puppy all his meals in the carrier, making sure to put the food bowl all the way at the back. Leave the door open until your puppy goes in and out with no problem. Put his familiar blanket in the carrier and hide one or two treats in its folds. If he lies down on the blanket of his own accord to take a nap, leave the door open for the time being. Once he accepts the carrier as the most natural thing in the world, place a favorite treat in it. While your puppy is feasting, close the door and put the carrier in the car. Be consistent and have patience.

❓ The breeder wants to wait until the puppy is 12 weeks old before letting us take him home. Do you see any problem with this?

The best time for adoption is when the puppies are eight to nine weeks old. This is because the puppy has to acclimate to a new environment without his littermates and mother during the socialization stage, which lasts only until the 14th week. If he misses this stage, he may have problems with strangers later on.

❓ Our puppy piddles every time he greets someone. Is it possible to put a stop to this?

This behavior is called submissive urination. It is characteristic of dogs that are extremely submissive. It can be caused by an innate temperament flaw, excessively harsh early training, or an extremely dominant personality in the person greeting him. Be more subdued and lower your voice. Call the puppy over before he submits and quickly give him a treat without saying a word. When he leaves, turn away and do not pay any more attention to him. In time he will become more confident. Visitors should not pay attention to him or speak to him. If he still piddles on occasion, ignore it completely and don't let him watch when you clean it up.

❓ What is meant by a dominant dog?

Basically, a dominant dog is friendly without fawning. He is not hostile or aggressive. He radiates calm and authority. Other dogs acknowledge that he is higher ranking by acting submissively toward him. He holds his head and tail high. Some dog owners think that their dog is dominant if he does what he wants when on a leash, shows aggression, or doesn't follow orders. As a rule, though, a dog like this is just badly trained. A dominant dog has no need for loud or physical confrontations.

❓ When should you use a harness instead of a collar for a dog?

I recommend using a harness for miniature breeds, dogs with a thick neck, or dogs with medical problems affecting the neck. During training, though, I prefer a soft collar because the dog has an easier time understanding signals with a leash and collar than with a harness.

A Healthful Diet

What sort of diet will ensure that our four-legged friends

enjoy a long and healthy life? In this chapter, I'll pass along what

I have learned on this topic from my 30 years of experience.

A Dog Is What She Eats

The ideal dog is wiry, muscular, neither too fat nor too thin, with a thick, shiny coat and clear, bright eyes. A balanced diet contributes in large measure to this.

We determine for ourselves how we want to eat, but our dogs depend on our decisions and our knowledge.

Natural Diet

The dog is a carnivore. She has the teeth of a predator, designed primarily for seizing and tearing apart prey. A natural diet, then, is geared toward prey animals. Their flesh provides the protein and fat, the bones supply calcium, the blood contains sodium, and the liver and kidneys are a source of fat-soluble vitamins; water-soluble vitamins can be found in the gut and its contents. The wolf, ancestor of our dogs, also eats fruits, grasses, roots, and leaves as well as the excrement of other animals and other sorts of scraps.

Too much grain is unhealthy: The dog's body is adapted to a high-protein diet, which means primarily meat. Dogs who are fed a mixed diet containing a high percentage of grain often develop digestive problems because the grain doesn't stimulate the gastric mucosa to produce enough hydrochloric acid. As a result, the stomach contents cannot be properly digested. That's why I recommend that if you give your dog grains, you never feed them along with meat.

Commercial Food Quality

Commercial dog food comes as dry (kibble) or moist (canned) food. Quality varies from manufacturer to manufacturer. For the most part, though, a "complete and balanced diet," according to the information on the package, provides all the nutrients the dog needs.

Chewing on something is not only fun, but also feels good when the dog is teething and her gums are sore.

Paying close attention: Something's going on here, and it could be very interesting.

Inferior commercial food consists primarily of grains, and the quality of the protein labeled as "animal by-products" is impossible to determine. When you buy commercial food, pay particular attention to the list of ingredients. The more accurately percentages are given for individual ingredients, the better. Of course, commercial dog food has been highly processed, cooked, and preserved. Processed food like this lacks the nutritional value of fresh food. That's why, for more than 30 years, I have been feeding my dogs raw meat, bones, vegetables, and appropriate snacks.

Homemade Food

The wolf doesn't just eat meat; he eats an animal "skin and all." Obviously, this type of natural diet is no longer feasible for most dog owners for aesthetic reasons alone. Therefore we have to assemble a diet from natural

ingredients that is as close as possible in composition to the diet of a wild canid. This should include the following basic components:

▶ meat
▶ bones and bone substitutes
▶ vegetables
▶ various food additives

Meat alone would be unhealthy for a dog because it contains too much phosphorus and too little calcium. A dog needs more calcium than phosphorus in her diet (ratio 1:1.2). In addition to feeding the dog bones, then, you must supplement her diet with calcium in other forms (see Bones, page 64). Suitable meats include beef, lamb, horse, game, and fish. Lean muscle meat has a high protein content and is easily digestible. Head meat and stew meat are higher in fat and have more connective tissue. Poultry (muscle meat) has high-quality protein while being low in fat. Organ meats (liver, heart, kidneys, spleen, lungs, tripe), which contain special vitamins and trace elements, should make up no more than 5 percent of the meat per meal because they are very high in phosphorus. With liver, there is a risk of supplying too much vitamin A. Tripe is not a good source of protein, contains a lot of connective tissue, and is difficult to digest. Different types and mixtures of frozen, minced meat are available commercially; these are fed at room temperature along with the water produced when they thaw.

TIP

Feeding on Vacation

When you travel on vacation, it's usually impossible to give your dog homemade food. I suggest you take along dry food instead of cans because it is easier to handle. Just make sure to switch to the unfamiliar food a few days before the trip so your dog can get used to it.

To keep your puppy healthy, feed her **a balanced diet**. Then she will develop beautifully both physically and mentally.

Caution! You should never feed your dog raw pork, because it can contain the Aujeszky's disease (pseudorabies) virus, which is fatal for dogs.

Bones supply more than just calcium for the dog; they are also a source of many other minerals. Raw, meaty brisket bones from calves or lambs are easily digested, provided the dog is at least the size of a Standard Dachshund, has healthy teeth, and has finished teething; just don't overdo it. Puppies or older dogs who have a hard time chewing and digesting bones must be given bone meal (it cannot have been heated; otherwise it loses its value),

The puppy attacks a mountain of food. It's better to divide the daily ration into four meals.

ground raw bones, eggshells, or calcium nitrate (absorbed better by the body than calcium carbonate) as a substitute or supplement.

Vegetables of many types, raw and finely chopped (almost pureed), are an excellent addition to the diet. Vary the mixture according to seasonal availability. Because plant cell walls are destroyed by chopping, the dog can easily digest the nutritious contents (vitamins, minerals, and trace elements). At the same time, she gets her dietary fiber. The vegetable mixture should consist primarily of an assortment of leafy greens, such as lettuce, arugula, spinach, dandelion greens, collard greens, and mustard greens. You can supplement this with your choice of other vegetables, for instance kohlrabi, cauliflower, celery, leeks, and Brussels sprouts. Carrots should make up one-third of any vegetable mixture, because they contain fiber that is beneficial for the intestinal flora and provide essential beta-carotene.

Caution! Raw potatoes, raw green beans, chili peppers, onions, and eggplants contain toxic substances.

Fruit of any kind, except grapes and raisins, in small amounts is a good between-meal snack.

Fats and oils are not only a source of energy, but are also essential nutrients. Vegetable oils contain a high percentage of unsaturated fatty acids. These are good for the dog's skin and coat.

Fats aid the absorption of fat-soluble vitamins and improve food intake. You can meet the dog's requirement for fats by feeding meat with a fat content of 10 to 15 percent and supplementing the diet with essential fatty acids like safflower oil, which is high in linoleic acid (72 percent).

Dairy products are something that many dogs love and can digest, whereas others have problems (diarrhea) with them because of their high lactose content. Adding a little milk to the dog's

are unable to digest cellulose, because their short digestive tracts and intestinal flora are not equipped to handle it. In commercial dog food, grain is broken down by heating and converted to starch so the dog can use it. To meet my dogs' minimal requirement for carbohydrates, I give them a slice of stale bread, a "cottage cheese breakfast" with rolled oats and coconut flakes, or homemade

DID YOU KNOW THAT...

...the dog's stomach is enormous?

Relative to body weight, it is eight times as large as a horse's stomach! This means the dog, like the wolf, can consume large quantities of food. Wolves need to do this because they don't make a kill every day, and when they return from the hunt, the pups and old wolves left behind induce them to regurgitate part of their food by muzzle nudging.

water will encourage reluctant drinkers to increase their water intake, if this is necessary for medical reasons. Soured milk products such as buttermilk, kefir, and yogurt are easy to digest because part of the lactose has been converted to lactic acid. Cheese cubes, popular as food rewards, are also easily digested; so is cottage cheese with a little honey and a raw egg yolk.

Carbohydrates are present in rolled oats, wheat flakes, rice, bread, zwieback, dog biscuits, and dog food flakes. A dog doesn't need very much. By nature, dogs

dog biscuits, but I feed these separately from the meat meals.

Food supplements: Depending on the dog's age or medical needs, her diet of meat, bones, and vegetables can be supplemented with a commercial mineral mixture that promotes healthy physical development. Ask your veterinarian for advice. Flaxseed oil or omega-3 fatty acids in the form of fish oil can supplement the essential fatty acids described on page 64. So, too, can algae such as spirulina in powder or tablet form.

BARF

The acronym BARF stands for biologically appropriate raw foods (or, as some have dubbed it, "bones and raw foods"). In 1993, the Australian veterinarian Dr. Ian Billinghurst published his findings on this feeding method. The BARF concept can be traced to a biologically appropriate diet, like the one I have been using for my dogs for more than 30 years. You do not need tables or scientific calculations to feed your dog a BARF diet. For a dog to be properly nourished with the BARF method, the ingredients must meet her nutritional requirements. These depend on her age and weight. Choose raw, fresh, natural products, and use my recipes (given later in the chapter) to help you determine the ratio of ingredients in the mixture. You can find additional information on the Internet (see Addresses, page 141).

Our four-legged friends have different ideas about what tastes good. Dogs usually prefer water from a pond to chlorinated tap water.

▼

Good Nutrition Makes a Great Dog

The first requirement for the healthy physical development of your puppy is a balanced diet. Responsible dog owners know that.

For the first four weeks of life, the sole source of nutrition for puppies is their mother's milk. After the fourth to fifth week, mother wolves supplement their milk by regurgitating predigested meat from prey animals for their pups, something our mother dogs rarely do. Beginning around the fourth to fifth week of life, breeders start giving their well-nourished puppies a special puppy formula and then, later on, gruel in addition to their mother's milk. The little ones also start eating tiny portions of finely minced, lean beef.

The Right Puppy Food

The puppies are weaned and eating solid food no later than eight weeks of age, at which time they are ready for adoption. Even before you bring your puppy home, you should decide what to feed her. But first, there are a few things you need to consider: Find out what constitutes high-quality commercial puppy food (see page 61). If you intend to prepare the puppy's food yourself, then you need an adequate understanding of her nutritional needs as well as which ingredients to use and how to prepare the food properly.

Making your dog's food is time consuming, but it can also be very gratifying. Of course, opening a can or a package of commercial food is faster. If you decide to prepare the food yourself, you need to find out whether you can get fresh meat in your neighborhood and how it is sold. Was the meat butchered under quality-controlled conditions overseen by food inspectors? Is the meat really fresh? Was frozen meat stored properly? Another point to consider is the price. Compare feeding options by calculating the cost for one day's worth of food.

In my experience, feeding fresh meat is cheapest if you can buy it at a good price. Ultimately, though, every dog owner has to decide which feeding method is best for his or her own puppy.

A good breeder will give you a detailed feeding schedule and a few days' supply of whatever food the puppy is accustomed to. A discussion with the breeder will help you decide what's best to feed your puppy over the coming weeks. In the end, though, you'll be able to tell by looking at her whether or not she is thriving on the diet you're giving her, or if something doesn't agree with her.

Feeding Tips

▶ **1** **Bowls:** A raised feeder with adjustable height is perfect for dogs who eat too fast. This way, they eat more calmly and don't swallow as much air.

▶ **2** **Bones:** Dogs love to chew on raw bones; besides, this inhibits the buildup of tartar.

▶ **3** **Water:** A ceramic bowl keeps fresh water cool longer. The dog must always have ready access to drinking water.

What and When to Feed

Until the puppy reaches six months of age, her daily food ration should be divided into four smaller meals. From six months to a year, she can manage on two or three larger portions. The puppy's stomach still can't handle large amounts of food. Besides, an overfilled stomach would put too much of a strain on the back muscles, which are not yet fully developed; this could lead to swayback, among other problems.

The first meal of the day is determined by your schedule, but it should not be later than 8 A.M. Since grains should never be fed together with meat—and the dog doesn't need very much grain, anyway—I use it for my puppies' "cottage cheese breakfast": depending on the size of the puppy, about 2.5 to 5 ounces (75 to 150 g) of low-fat cottage cheese, about 1 heaping tablespoon rolled oats, 1 heaping teaspoon coconut flakes, 1 teaspoon wheat germ, 1 teaspoon honey, 1 teaspoon bee pollen, 1 teaspoon safflower oil or sunflower oil, 1/2 teaspoon finely crushed eggshells, and every other day a raw egg yolk. The puppy will also appreciate a little finely grated apple (unpeeled). If the gruel is too dry, thin it with a little plain yogurt or milk. This highly nutritious, natural breakfast is also good for puppies who are given commercial dog food for the rest of the day. For these dogs, especially, the cottage cheese breakfast is a valuable supplement to their diet.

The next three meals for my puppies consist of a meat mush that I prepare according to the following recipe: 75 percent (of the total amount of mush) minced, raw beef (muscle meat or head meat); 20 percent vegetables (see page 64), blanched (boiled quickly) at first, then raw once the puppy is used to them (the vegetables must be pureed). Depending on the season, mix in 1 tablespoon of finely chopped, fresh, young leafy greens or wild garlic. Add 1 teaspoon of cold-pressed safflower

oil and, in the winter, another 1 teaspoon of cod-liver oil. If you don't give your dog a cottage cheese breakfast, then three times a week put a raw egg yolk over the food (egg whites must always be cooked before feeding them to your dog). Supplement this with a multivitamin/mineral mixture suitable for the dog, which will provide adequate amounts of calcium and other essential vitamins and minerals; ask your veterinarian to suggest one (see Food supplements, page 65).

Tip: If you give your puppy commercial food, it's best to continue using the one recommended by the breeder; your puppy will already be used to it.

How to Feed

Free-choice feeding: Should food always be readily available so the dog can eat whenever she wants, or is it better to feed her at specific times? This question has frequently been the subject of heated discussions. As far as I'm concerned, there are several arguments against free-choice feeding:

▸ Most dogs suffer from an excess of food as it is. Overfed and overweight dogs are plagued by physical and psychological ailments.
▸ The digestive organs cannot empty properly between meals and get a chance to rest.

TIP

Stick to the Menu

If you're constantly changing your dog's diet, you risk raising a picky eater. Should it be necessary to switch foods for medical reasons, mix a small amount of the new food in with the dog's current food, gradually increasing the amount day by day until it replaces the "old" food.

Feeding Guidelines

Pay attention to the following when feeding your puppy:

- ○ Always feed the puppy at the same time and in the same place.

- ○ She should feel secure and, above all, content where you feed her.

- ○ See to it that nobody disturbs her when she eats; this goes for the whole family, including the children.

- ○ Divide her daily ration into portions so that she cannot overeat at any meal.

- ○ Take her food away as soon as she leaves the bowl.

▸ During training, a dog like this is more difficult to motivate and less responsive to positive reinforcement because she is already "full."

▸ So-called free-choice feeding works only with dry food (kibble), because fresh meat attracts flies in warm weather and also begins to spoil.

▸ If you have several dogs, the greedy ones would soon overeat and get fat.

Rationed feeding works with all types of food. The dog's rectum adjusts to certain feeding times, making it easier for you to plan for "walkies." With punctual feedings, you also prevent the dog from begging. Put the food bowl down in front of her and watch her as she eats. She should eat rapidly with a good appetite. If she doesn't do that, or if she even walks away from her bowl, take the food away. This is an effective method for dealing with poor eaters; besides, it's a good way to monitor how much she eats. At the next meal, give your dog her normal portion of food again. Under no circumstances should you change the composition of the food, say by mixing in special treats. Otherwise, your clever dog might make a habit of rejecting her food at first in an attempt to get a few extra tidbits.

Tip: Refusal to eat can also be an indication of illness. Usually, however, there are other signs associated with this (for example apathy or fever) (see page 86).

How much to feed: If your puppy leaves a little food in her bowl, feed her exactly this much less at the next meal. If she still seems hungry after a meal, and if her weight allows it (see Weight Monitoring, page 71), give her a little more, but not until the next meal.

Where to feed: Always feed the puppy in the same place, somewhere she can eat without being disturbed. After each feeding, wash the bowl with hot water. Put leftover food in the garbage, not back in the refrigerator. The puppy must always have access to fresh water. Naturally, the water bowl is washed every day with hot water (see page 68).

Food quality: Food must always be perfectly fresh. Homemade food and food that has been sitting around too long can spoil and cause diarrhea. Once you open a can of food, remove what's left from the can and store it in a covered plastic container in the refrigerator. Food taken directly from the refrigerator will make the puppy sick. She'll really enjoy her food if you warm it up slightly, because then the flavors are more intense. Pour warm water over the kibble and let it soak briefly.

Weight Monitoring

In the first weeks, check once a week to find out whether or not your puppy is continuing to gain weight. If her weight is increasing, that lets you know you are giving her a good, healthy diet.

Tip: Overfeeding puppies of large breeds between the third and sixth months can make them grow too quickly and cause permanent damage. Because their young bones are still soft and pliable, placing too much weight on them can lead to later misalignments or aggravate conditions such as congenital hip dysplasia.

Weighing: This is quite easy to do. Stand on your bathroom scale and weigh yourself. Then pick up your puppy and stand on the scale with her. The difference between this new reading and your weight is the weight of the puppy. The scale alone isn't much help in determining whether your puppy is overfed or underfed. First you have to know your puppy's normal weight for her age. Here are some guidelines:

Medium-sized breeds: The end-of-month weight for a medium-sized breed with an adult weight of 44 pounds (20 kg):

    2nd month = 10 pounds (4.4 kg)
    3rd month = 16 pounds (7.4 kg)
    4th month = 23 pounds (10.4 kg)
    6th month = 31 pounds (14.0 kg)
    12th month = 42 pounds (19.0 kg).

Healthy puppies must gain
weight steadily; otherwise
there's something wrong.

Large breeds: The end-of-month weight for a large breed with an adult weight of about 77 pounds (35 kg):

    2nd month = 15 pounds (7.0 kg)
    3rd month = 27 pounds (12.2 kg)
    4th month = 37 pounds (16.8 kg)
    6th month = 50 pounds (22.8 kg)
    12th month = 66 pounds (29.8 kg).

You could almost use a letter scale to weigh a tiny puppy like this. ▶

Watching her figure: As a concerned dog owner, you will soon learn to judge the nutritional status of your adult dog. Stand behind your dog and place your hands on either side of her rib cage. By applying slight pressure, you should be able to feel the ribs easily. If you have to press hard with your fingers before you feel the ribs, your dog is overweight. People often talk about "puppy fat," which the puppy outgrows. That holds true only until about the twelfth to fourteenth week of life. After that the puppy should be wiry, muscular, and always a little bit hungry.

Subject: Dog Poop

In a healthy puppy, the feces are egg shaped and elastic, not hard and crumbly or mushy.

The color depends on the food. With a balanced diet, the feces are brown to dark brown. They can be light gray if your puppy is getting too many bones, or yellowish with too much milk. Nearly black, greasy feces occur when dogs are fed exclusively on liver. If the puppy has diarrhea without blood, stop feeding her for a day. If the diarrhea continues or if it is bloody, take the puppy to the veterinarian immediately.

MY PET

How Secure Does Your Puppy Feel in Her Environment?

After the puppy has adjusted to living in your home, she may want to explore her immediate surroundings, too. Here is an opportunity for you to test your puppy to see how secure or insecure she feels in her environment.

The test begins:

Gradually introduce your puppy to unfamiliar adults, children, and other dogs. How does she behave when there's noise from traffic? Observe your puppy's behavior. In which situations does she seem anxious? When does she get frightened? Take several days to do the test. Do not overtax the puppy with too many new impressions.

My test results:

You can't say that this dog is stealing. Thanks to her owner's forgetfulness, she has discovered the sausage and "appropriated" it.

Volume of feces: Your puppy's feces reveal a great deal about the quality of her food. The more "indigestible" matter contained in your dog's food (possibly cheap commercial food), the more feces she produces. If the volume of feces is as large as the amount of food, though, you should take your puppy to the veterinarian.

Special Problems

Spoiled, moldy foods contain toxins that can produce severe symptoms of poisoning in the dog. Storing kibble and other foods under warm, humid conditions encourages a rapid buildup of these poisons. As a scavenger, the dog can certainly handle some harmful organisms with her gastric and bile acids, but these do not neutralize the toxins. If you notice any mold, you must dispose of the entire package as a precaution.

Eating grass can occur for various reasons. The most common cause is digestive upset, often triggered by excess gastric acid. The dog then vomits the grass along with yellowish foam. Dogs often supplement their diet by eating tender young grass, but they don't vomit that up again. My German Shepherd, for example, loves to eat the dried leaves of our Virginia creeper.

Eating feces (coprophagy) may be a sign of a dietary deficiency. If your dog eats her own feces or those of another animal, she may be suffering from a digestive enzyme deficiency. If she eats the dung of horses, cattle, or sheep, this can mean a protein or vitamin B deficiency. Check the composition of the dog food. If everything is in order, you must resort to training measures. Incidentally, a mother dog eats the feces of her puppies, but this is a normal behavior.

Grooming and Health Care

Regular grooming is an important part of caring for
your pet's health. And if he gets sick, don't delay—take him
to the veterinarian as quickly as possible.

The Well-Groomed Dog— Beautiful and Healthy

From the time your puppy is small, get him used to seeing grooming rituals as something positive. A gentle brush massage followed by words of praise from you and a treat for good behavior are guaranteed to make your puppy happy.

The benefits of regular grooming are more than just good hygiene and a beautiful coat. You will also spot signs of disease more quickly. In addition, getting "up close and personal" with your dog has an important social component: Your dog learns to trust you. That's something he won't forget, even if he is sick and in pain and you have to handle him when he may not like it.

A Beautiful Coat

Dogs have many different types of coats—long coats (Collie), double coats (German Shepherd Dog), smooth coats (Boxer), wire coats (Fox Terrier), and coats that must be trimmed according to specific breed standards (Poodle). All dogs, except for those who are clipped, shed twice a year, which means they lose the old, dead hair. In dogs with a very dense undercoat (northern breeds), the hair is sometimes shed in large patches. You can make the process a little less abrupt if you brush your dog regularly.

Get your dog used to being groomed: Place a blanket on the table and put your puppy on it. Get him to lie down and relax by petting him and speaking to him in a soothing voice. As soon as he is thoroughly enjoying having you scratch his tummy, show him the brush and comb and let him sniff them. Begin to brush his coat very gently and without pressure, brushing in the direction of hair growth. After two or three brush strokes, praise him and give him a treat. Stop grooming at this point. The next day, try to brush him a little longer; you can also start using the comb carefully. During the entire procedure, be sure to stay relaxed.

This beautiful King Charles puppy is well groomed from head to toe. ▷

If you are too rough and impatient the first time you groom a puppy and hurt him, he will not look forward to being brushed and combed later on. Once the puppy realizes that the brush and comb feel good, though, and that he can expect treats during the process as well as when it's all over, he will be happy to trust you and enjoy having you groom him.

Bathing: A dog usually doesn't need to be bathed if he is combed and brushed regularly and lives in a clean home. If it becomes necessary, though, you'll need to use a moisturizing dog shampoo so that you don't destroy the

diet can cause a dull, brittle, dry, foul-smelling (rancid) coat along with dry, flaky skin. A balanced mineral supplement (from the veterinarian), brewer's yeast, egg yolks, or up to one tablespoon of safflower oil a day can help. It's best to take your pet to the veterinarian.

A Clean Nose

The leathery tip of the dog's nose (the "nose leather") should always be moist and clean. After your puppy has been digging in the yard, clean the nose leather with lukewarm water

Your puppy must enjoy having you groom him. **Stay calm and patient as you work.** If you are rushed and nervous, he will have a negative experience.

protective lipid layer of your dog's skin. Make sure that the dog's coat is dry before he goes outside, especially in winter. As soon as the weather warms up enough, you should encourage your puppy to splash around in shallow water (a kiddie pool) so that he'll learn to love the water. Regular swimming in summer is the best coat care. When the coat is dry after a swim, comb it lightly; give short-haired dogs a massage by brushing the coat against the direction of growth.

Pathological changes in the coat: Nutritional deficiencies or an improper

and, if it is too dry, lubricate it with petroleum jelly to keep it soft and prevent chapping.

If the dog has a watery, clear nasal discharge associated with fever, or a purulent, mucous, or bloody discharge, consult the veterinarian without delay.

Lip Care

Normally, the lips of a dog are firm and closed. In some breeds (for example the Great Dane and Mastiff), breeders have "succeeded" in producing pendulous lips.

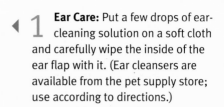

Ear Care: Put a few drops of ear-cleaning solution on a soft cloth and carefully wipe the inside of the ear flap with it. (Ear cleansers are available from the pet supply store; use according to directions.)

Dental Checkup: Regularly check the puppy's teeth for foreign objects and tartar. Watch for any pathological changes of the gums and throat.

2 ▶

◀ 3 **Eye Care:** Remove crusty buildup from the corner of the eye with a soft, damp cloth. Purulent discharge or conjunctivitis requires veterinary care (see page 78).

Paw Care: Regularly check the sensitive pads and the area between the toes for foreign bodies. Lubricate the paw pads with petroleum jelly (see page 79).

4 ▶

In the winter, the puppy should not eat ice.

Abnormal signs include progressive clouding or changes in the color of the eye, purulent discharge, inflammation of the conjunctiva, and bulging eyes. Then a visit to the veterinarian is in order.

Dental Care

Check your puppy's teeth regularly for the presence of tartar and foreign objects caught between the teeth. If you start early getting your puppy used to having his teeth cleaned with a toothbrush and toothpaste made especially for dogs, he will put up with it once he's fully grown. Make sure he is not missing any teeth; dogs have 28 deciduous (baby) teeth and 42 permanent (adult) teeth.

Ear Care

Dogs have erect ("pricked") ears, erect ears with bent tips ("semi-pricked" ears), or pendulous ("drop") ears. They must be cleaned regularly to remove dirt and earwax. To do this, use a special ear-cleaning solution (from the pet supply store), which is warmed slightly and applied to the ear. Drop ears need special care, because their shape prevents them from drying out adequately on their own. Without proper care, this can lead to ear infections. The dog first indicates an ear problem by cautiously scratching at his ears, then by shaking his head vigorously and tilting it in the direction of the affected ear.

The natural outcome is that these dogs more or less inevitably slobber. Bits of food and dirt accumulate in the lip folds and, without proper care, will get stuck there and be impossible for the dog to clean out with his tongue. This often leads to the development of what is known as lip fold dermatitis or cheilitis. Regular cleansing with lukewarm water and the occasional application of a bit of petroleum jelly to encrusted areas prevent this sort of problem.

Eye Care

The eyes must be clear. The eyelids should close tightly and keep dirt from getting into the eye. Remove crusty buildup from the corners of your puppy's eyes every morning with a damp cloth.

Paw and Nail Care

Paws: The paw pads are, so to speak, the soles of the dog's feet. Care for them by washing them off occasionally, making sure you get between the toes, and lubricating them with petroleum jelly. In the winter, make sure to wash road salt off the paws. Rub a little paw wax into the pads or use a protective spray (from the pet store) to safeguard against this aggressive salt. In snowy weather, dogs with especially furry feet can develop painful ice clumps between their toes. Rubbing in some paw wax or trimming the hair helps prevent this. If your dog accompanies you when you're bicycling on paved streets, his paws can be abraded so badly that he comes home with bloody feet. Paw injuries can lead to infections or calluses.

Nails: Under normal conditions, the dog will wear down his nails naturally if he gets enough exercise. However, in many breeds, especially the larger ones, improper diet may lead to the development of such severe joint problems, which may prevent normal wear. Have the veterinarian show you how to trim the nails.

The Genitals

Inspect the female's vagina regularly for any unusual discharge. A bloody vaginal discharge is normal for females

1 **Coat care for beginners:** Brushing stimulates the sebaceous glands in the skin, giving the coat a beautiful sheen. The first time you try to groom the puppy, simply get him used to being touched with the brush.

2 **Coat care for old hands:** The puppy now knows that brushing is nice and that maybe he'll even get a treat after his "beauty treatment." He lies on his side, completely relaxed, and enjoys the gentle massage.

Health Check

The earlier you notice any signs of illness in your puppy, the more likely it is that he'll recover. Here's how to recognize a healthy puppy:

○ When he's awake, your puppy is cheerful, carefree, inquisitive, and always ready to play.

○ His body is muscular, neither too thin nor too fat (see page 71).

○ His coat is clean and shiny.

○ His skin is smooth and supple; there are no swellings beneath the skin, and, of course, there are no parasites.

○ Legs and paws are flexible and cause him no apparent pain when he walks or runs.

○ The puppy moves smoothly in all gaits with no sign of impediment.

○ The paw pads are not sensitive when you touch them.

○ The ears are clean and odorless.

○ The eyes are clear and bright.

○ The teeth are white and undamaged; no teeth are missing (see page 78).

○ The gums and tongue are moist and pink.

in heat. If you keep the dog indoors, you can get diapers to prevent blood from dripping on the floor. Check the testicles of male dogs for swelling or abnormalities. Flushing the skin covering the penis (the "sheath") can prevent infections in males. Discuss this with your veterinarian. If your puppy has only one testicle or none at all, take him to the veterinarian. Testicles that remain within the abdomen ("undescended testicles") can cause problems for the dog later.

Rear End, Urine, and Feces

Anus and anal glands: Don't hesitate to check under your dog's tail frequently. Usually, though, the dog takes care of this area himself. On either side of the anus are the anal glands, which secrete a smelly substance when the dog defecates. This is the dog's individual "scent," and dogs use it to recognize each other. Always keep the anus and anal glands clean. If necessary, wipe them off with a damp towel and lubricate them occasionally with petroleum jelly. If the openings of the anal glands become clogged, it can lead to impaction and inflammation, which must be treated by a veterinarian.

Urine: Urine should come out in a stream when the dog urinates, not just a trickle. The color should be light yellow to dark yellow.

Feces: Check the dog's feces daily. They should be sausage shaped, solid, compact, and firm but not too hard. If the dog has diarrhea without blood, stop feeding for one day. Check to see if his food could have caused the diarrhea (see page 72).

Health Care: Prevention and Treatment

Giving your puppy a healthful diet, regular grooming, plenty of exercise, and appropriate activities is the best way to keep him healthy. If he still gets sick, you must take him to the veterinarian without delay.

In your daily interactions with your puppy as well as when you are grooming him, you can quickly tell if he has a problem or might be coming down with something.

Signs of Illness

The following changes will be obvious, even to a layman:

Behavioral changes: The puppy seems sad, listless, sulky, or ill-tempered. He keeps changing position; he is jumpy and very restless. He wanders back and forth aimlessly, whines, cries, howls, or seems especially anxious. He appears dazed and/or indifferent to his surroundings. His gaze is expressionless, and he has a slow, dragging gait. He sleeps constantly. The puppy occasionally seems disoriented, faints, or has dizzy spells.

Bodily changes: There are noticeable changes in the shape or position of the bones. The dog suddenly loses or gains a lot of weight. The skin is taut. The puppy's hair is falling out, or his coat is dull.

Skin changes: The puppy's visible mucous membranes (conjunctiva of the eyeball and oral mucosa of the mouth) are noticeably pale or discolored (see Checklist, page 80). The skin of the inner thighs and the belly is discolored. The skin is dry, hard, hot, or cold. The skin gives off a foul smell. The skin is sensitive to pain or exhibits doughy swellings.

Body temperature and pulse: The dog's normal temperature is between 99.5 and 102°F (37.5 and 39°C) for adults, and up to 103°F (39.5°C) for puppies.

The pulse in larger dogs is 70 to 130 beats per minute, in smaller breeds up to 180, and in puppies up to 220.

> **TIP**
>
> ## Worm Infestation
>
> A puppy with a severe worm infestation can lose a great deal of blood and become malnourished. Other signs of infection are diarrhea, vomiting, and rump-rubbing ("scooting") due to anal itching. If you see blood in the feces, it could be roundworms. Black feces suggest hookworms and can be an indication of intestinal bleeding.

The pulse can also be increased by anxiety, fright, happiness, and prolonged, strenuous physical activity or other types of exertion. You can feel the pulse on the inner side of the thigh. The pulse can slow down if the dog has been poisoned or speed up if he is suffering from fever, heart failure, or blood loss. The respiration rate of a dog at rest is 10 to 30 breaths per minute.

Puppies show that they are sick by **changes in their behavior.** That's when a trip to the veterinarian is absolutely necessary.

Taking the dog's temperature: Use a clinical thermometer that allows you to measure the temperature in the dog's ear. This method is quicker and much easier than taking the temperature rectally.

If the dog lies around listlessly, he could be sick.

▼

Visiting the Veterinarian

When a pet has to go to the veterinarian, most owners are upset and have a hard time answering any of the doctor's questions. So here's my tip: Jot down the symptoms that you noticed in your puppy. You should also be able to describe the dog's feces and urine. Without details like these, it is sometimes impossible for the veterinarian to diagnose the problem quickly.

Disease Prevention

Deworming: Deworming must begin in puppyhood, because puppies can be infected prenatally with round-worm larvae transmitted through their mother's blood. After birth, the puppies can be infected again through their mother's milk. For this reason, treatment of roundworms (ascarids belong to this group) must begin when the puppies are two weeks old and should continue at 14-day intervals until they are 12 weeks old.

Adult dogs, on the other hand, are no longer dewormed today "just in case," but only if worms—no matter what kind—are discovered in a stool sample.

In any event, the dog must be wormed before a scheduled vaccination; other-wise the protection conferred by the vaccine cannot develop sufficiently.

Vaccinations: In dogs, as with us, there are a number of often fatal infectious diseases for which vaccines have been developed. Every puppy should receive the so-called "core" vaccinations, because they can save his life.

VACCINATIONS AGAINST DANGEROUS INFECTIOUS DISEASES	
AGE AT VACCINATION	**VACCINE**
7–8 weeks	distemper, parvovirus, hepatitis
11–12 weeks	distemper, parvovirus, hepatitis, rabies
15 weeks	distemper, parvovirus, hepatitis

Tip: At present, there is considerable discussion about the conventional vaccination schedule and the need for boosters. Vaccines are now available that confer protection significantly longer than those previously recommended and prescribed by law (for example, rabies). Find out the details and decide about your puppy's vaccination schedule after consulting with your veterinarian.

The most dangerous infectious diseases include:

▶ canine distemper,
▶ hepatitis (infectious inflammation of the liver),
▶ leptospirosis (also called Stuttgart disease),
▶ rabies, and
▶ canine parvovirus infection.

Puppies do acquire some natural immunity through their mother's milk, but this effect lasts only a short time. When the puppies are six to eight weeks old, protection drops off sharply. The puppy receives the core vaccines in two or more doses approximately four weeks apart. Full protection takes one to two weeks to develop after the vaccination. During this period, the puppy should be kept away from animals suspected of being sick.

The Most Dangerous Infectious Diseases

Without vaccination, these infectious diseases are often fatal for the dog.

Canine distemper, also called hardpad disease. Symptoms: attacks of fever, vomiting, diarrhea, nasal discharge that is watery at first and then becomes purulent, cold-like symptoms, pneumonia.

Additional symptoms include avoidance of light (photophobia); purulent conjunctivitis; blindness; pustulation; reddening of the skin of the inner thighs and belly; dull, shaggy coat; and a range of neurological disorders, from muscle twitching to paralysis. Signs of the disease vary and can occur one after another or all at once.

Regular vaccinations are an **important part of** preventive care. They can save a life!

Infectious canine hepatitis. Symptoms: fever, depression, loss of appetite, tonsillitis, conjunctivitis, difficulty swallowing, bleeding from the mucous membranes, and temporary clouding of the cornea ("blue eye") in mild cases. There are catastrophic forms of the disease ending in sudden death; often this leads to the mistaken suspicion that the dog died of poisoning.

Leptospirosis, also called Stuttgart disease. Symptoms: fever, systemic disorders, weakness, reddening of the mucous membranes, jaundice resulting from liver damage and destruction of red blood cells, uncontrollable vomiting, diarrhea, dehydration. There are mild as well as fatal forms of the disease.

Rabies. Symptoms: The classic form of the disease is divided into three phases. First, the animal's behavior changes. He becomes shy, seeks solitude, refuses to obey, appears nervous, and snaps at "flies." In the second phase, called *furious rabies,* the animal becomes aggressive; additional symptoms include restlessness, biting and attacking without provocation, drooling, frenzied behavior, and abnormal appetite (eating straw, textiles, wood, feces). Phase three is marked by exhaustion and paralysis, ending with the death of the animal.

There is also a paralytic form of the disease known as *dumb rabies,* which is characterized by apathy, an expressionless stare, paralysis and drooping of the lower jaw, and a hoarse bark.

Canine parvovirus infection, also called parvo. Symptoms: watery, foul-smelling, occasionally bloody diarrhea; vomiting; loss of appetite; lethargy; severe dehydration; myocarditis. Frequently fatal in young puppies.

External Parasites

Fleas: Fleas are certainly the most familiar of the dog's parasites. Although, in my opinion, a healthy dog certainly has the right to a few fleas of his own, they can be a real nuisance, because fleas never travel alone. In a massive infestation, the dog can develop itching, allergic reactions to flea saliva, crusty skin lesions, and hair loss. Adult fleas live in the dog's coat and suck blood from his skin. They need the blood to lay their eggs. The flea eggs drop off the dog and land wherever the dog rests (such as his basket, carpet, or upholstered furniture), where they develop into adults. Adult fleas make up no more than 1 to 5 percent of the flea population; this means that, in addition to controlling fleas on the dog, you also have to treat the dog's environment, because that's where the flea's developmental stages—egg, larva, pupa—are found.

2 **Administering eyedrops:** With the thumb of your left hand, gently pull down the lower eyelid while holding the puppy's head steady. Squeeze the eyedrops onto the lower lid using your right hand.

1 **Taking the dog's temperature:** Lubricate the thermometer with petroleum jelly, insert into the rectum, and hold it until you get a reading.

3 **Applying a bandage:** To stop bleeding, it is sometimes necessary to apply a bandage. Work calmly and patiently when you do this.

To control fleas on the dog, you can use modern "spot-on" preparations that are applied topically, baths, powders, sprays, and special flea collars. The immature fleas can be tackled with insect growth regulators (spray, fogger, tablets). The dog's environment, especially the places where he lies, must be vacuumed, washed, and treated with a flea-control spray.

Ticks: Ticks are also bloodsuckers. They are found primarily in woods with heavy underbrush and on the edges of fields and meadows. They are most active in May/June and September/October. The brown dog tick was introduced from the tropics and, like other tick species, transmits a number of serious diseases, including Lyme disease (borreliosis), babesiosis, ehrlichiosis, and Rocky Mountain spotted fever. Preventive measures include tick collars, spot-on preparations, and sprays. My tip: Occasionally add half a clove of crushed garlic to the puppy's food, if he tolerates it. After every walk in the woods or fields, the dog must be brushed, rubbed down, and checked for ticks. To remove a tick using tick forceps, grasp its body close to the dog's skin and twist gently as you pull it out. Don't dab the tick with oil, gasoline, or glue—the tick could rupture, increasing the risk of infection.

Lice: Rare in well-groomed domestic dogs, lice are found primarily in stray dogs. Lice cause restlessness, itching, damaged skin, oozing or crusty skin lesions, and hair loss. Unlike fleas, lice and their offspring can't survive without the dog. They are found primarily on the dog's upper lip, the

THE MOST COMMON HEALTH PROBLEMS

Signs	Additional Symptoms	Possible Diseases
Not eating	diarrhea, vomiting, fever, apathy, thirst	viral infection, metritis (inflammation of the uterus), foreign body in the intestine
Not drinking	heavy drooling, coughing, gagging, swallowing for no reason	foreign body in the throat, pharyngeal paralysis
Drinking excessively	vomiting, abnormally low temperature, staggering, apathy	kidney damage (with uremia), diabetes, pyometra
Vomiting	bloody mucus, fever, not defecating, taut abdomen	gastritis, foreign body in the stomach, liver or kidney disease
Straining to defecate or urinate	mucus and blood coming from the anus, blood in the urine	constipation caused by ingested bones, urinary or bladder stones
Diarrhea	blood in the feces, vomiting, dehydration	worm infestation, gastrointestinal infection, poisoning, liver disease, pancreatic disease
Coughing	dry cough with gagging on phlegm, also dry cough with bloody mucus	tonsillitis, pharyngitis, or laryngitis (kennel cough)
Bad breath	drooling, excessive drinking, urine-like or foul mouth odor	tartar, periodontal disease, tooth abscess, gastritis, kidney disease
Shaking or tilting the head	foul-smelling ears, painful when scratched	foreign body in the ear, too much earwax, ear mites, inflammation
Scratching	pustules, hair loss, reddening of the skin, swelling	eczema, parasite infestation (fleas, ticks), allergy, tumor
Licking the anal area	dog rubs rear end on the ground ("scooting")	impacted anal glands, worm infestation
Limping	lameness and swelling, walks on three legs	sprain, joint or muscle injury or disease
Watery discharge from the eyes	purulent discharge, inflamed conjunctiva	inflammation, infection, foreign body in the eye, hereditary eye disease

base of the ear, and the neck. Their eggs (nits) are glued to the hairs of the coat. The best method for preventing lice is regular grooming. Lice can be controlled with powders or special baths (from the pet store).

Hair-follicle mites (*Demodex* mites) naturally reside in hair follicles and sebaceous (oil) glands. Problems arise only when a disorder of the dog's immune system leads to a massive increase in the mite population. Signs of infestation appear as hairless, reddened spots on the upper lip, eyelids, bridge of the nose, forehead, ears, front legs, or the webbing between the toes; there is scaling, but little itching. Young dogs and animals with a weakened immune system are primarily at risk. The parasites are transmitted by the mother when the puppies snuggle with her to nurse. When older dogs get sick, they were already infected as puppies. Mites are controlled with special baths, solutions, and/or injections (from the veterinarian) and by strengthening the dog's immune system.

Ear mites are spread by contact from dog to dog and also from cat to dog. The mites invade the external ear canal and the inside of the earflap. Signs of infection include intense itching and scratching, head shaking, rubbing the ear on the floor, increased production of earwax, inflammation of the ear canal, and the presence of dark brown, sandy or crumbly secretions. In severe cases, rupture of the eardrum, inflammation of the middle ear (otitis media), and deafness can result. Prevent infection by checking the ears regularly (see page 78). Treatment with a special medication to kill the mites (miticide) should be carried out only by a veterinarian.

Internal Parasites

Roundworms: These are by far the most common type of parasitic worm, and all puppies are assumed to be infected (see page 82). Roundworms are white, round in cross section, and look like spaghetti.

Make sure to keep your dog **free of parasites.** An infestation must be treated.

In nursing puppies, migration of the larvae throughout the body can result in lung damage and pneumonia. Signs of infection are coughing, nasal discharge, and vomiting. The puppy's belly is

This inflatable, soft collar prevents the dog from licking wounds and eczema.

swollen and tender ("potbelly"). The feces are loose and covered with mucus. Infected dogs lose weight, have no appetite, and become anemic. Worms can accumulate in the intestine and cause intestinal obstructions. Round-worm infection is prevented by systematic deworming of mother dogs and their puppies (see pages 81 and 82). Additional important

the feces. Dried tapeworm segments look like grains of rice stuck to the fur of the dog's hind legs and tail or found in his bed. Rigorous flea control prevents tapeworm infections. This parasitic infection is best treated by a veterinarian.

Exotic Parasites

Babesiosis (*piroplasmosis*) is caused by a blood parasite transmitted by tick bites. The parasite is common in

DID YOU KNOW THAT...

...you shouldn't put off going to the veterinarian?

The following symptoms require immediate attention: persistent or bloody vomiting or labored breathing (possible gastric torsion, also called "bloat"); blood in the urine or feces (serious disease or internal injuries); distinct change in behavior when urinating (kidney failure, an infection, or poisoning); disorientation, staggering, or collapse (disorders of the heart or brain, high blood pressure, or poisoning).

measures are regular fecal exams for adult dogs, proper disposal of feces, and good hygiene. It's best to discuss deworming with your veterinarian.

Tapeworms: The double-pored tapeworm, *Dipylideum caninum,* is the species most often found in dogs. Tapeworms are transmitted by fleas, which are hosts for the infectious stage. Tapeworms rarely cause serious illness, although sometimes the dog exhibits changes in appetite or diarrhea. Tape-worm segments are eliminated with

the northeastern parts of the United States. Symptoms: The dog is lethargic and weak, loses his appetite, and has a high fever, pale gums resulting from anemia, jaundice, and greenish-brown urine caused by the destruction of red blood cells. He loses weight and has difficulty breathing.

Babesiosis often results in the death of the dog because of kidney failure. To prevent infection, don't take your dog along on vacation to areas where this disease is prevalent, because unfortunately, our dogs are very susceptible to the pathogen. At present, no vaccine is available for use here. Your veterinarian will treat the disease with medications and may order blood transfusions, because the parasite destroys red blood cells.

Leishmaniasis: This infection is transmitted by bloodsucking sandflies. The disease often doesn't appear until months or years after the insect bites the dog. The parasite, prevalent in the Mediterranean region, has been introduced to North America and Europe. Infected dogs suffer from skin lesions and changes in the coat, including hair loss, severe dandruff, and ulceration; cracked and brittle nails; swollen lymph nodes; attacks of fever; weight loss; changes in appetite; nosebleeds; anemia; eye lesions; kidney failure; lameness; and tender abdomen caused by enlargement of the liver and spleen. Leishmaniasis is often fatal. As a preventive measure, you should not take your dog along with you to areas where the disease has been found. Veterinary treatment is prolonged and often unsuccessful. The medications used to treat this disease have numerous side effects.

Heartworm disease (*dirofilariasis*): Transmitted by mosquitoes, this parasitic worm lives in the heart and major pulmonary blood vessels of the dog. The disease was introduced from tropical areas of southern Europe and America by "canine tourists." Medications are available to prevent it as well as to treat it, but in some cases tangles of worms must be removed surgically from the blood vessels.

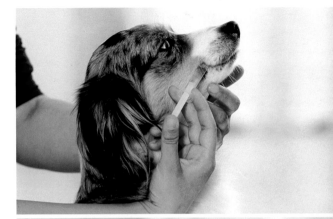

Administering medications

▶ 1 **Liquid medication:** Squirt it into the side of the dog's mouth using an oral syringe (without needle). Important: Tilt the puppy's head back slightly so that the medicine doesn't run out.

▶ 2 **Pills:** Place them as far back on the tongue as possible. Hold the dog's mouth closed with your hand until he swallows. Make sure to let him drink water afterward.

Spaying or Hormone Therapy?

Female dogs come into heat twice a year (see page 51). If you don't want to breed your dog or would like to keep her as part of a mixed multi-dog household, you must give some thought to preventing pregnancy. In addition, many dogs without access to a sexual partner undergo false pregnancy. They can develop pyometra, ovarian disease, and mammary tumors. There are two possible solutions to these problems:

Vaccinate your puppy to prevent him from being infected by diseased animals.

Have your dog spayed, or suppress her heat cycle by administering hormones.

Spaying: In spaying, the ovaries and uterus are surgically removed. Spaying is recommended at about six months of age, before the female's first heat. If done too early, though, spaying may increase the likelihood of growth problems as well as some cancers. Talk with your veterinarian about when to schedule the operation. The earlier the dog is spayed, the greater the protective benefits. However, spaying can have side effects. As with any surgery, there are certain risks associated with anesthesia. Sometimes, too, the incision heals slowly because the dog licks it, but you can tackle this problem by using an antiseptic spray and having the dog wear a T-shirt that covers the area of the incision.

About 10 days after the operation, the sutures are removed and the dog recovers. Occasionally, the dog experiences urinary incontinence, but this usually affects heavy dogs of large breeds, and with appropriate medications, can be quickly solved. In long-haired breeds there is sometimes an increase in the wooly undercoat; the coat becomes softer and more fleecy, more like puppy fur. When spayed females gain weight, it is because of the owner rather than the surgery. With controlled feeding, sufficient exercise, and plenty of activity, the problem will never arise.

All my females were and are spayed, and I have had no negative experiences with it. Unspayed females suffer sexual stress when they come into heat, and they cannot get rid of it by mating. During this period, many females

MY PET

Is Your Puppy Happy?

If a puppy is not happy, he shows it right away by his behavior. Watch your puppy closely and test him to see if he is contented. Pay special attention to the following positive behaviors described below.

The test begins:
- ○ The puppy moves around freely and naturally at home.
- ○ He has a good appetite.
- ○ He sleeps peacefully.
- ○ He is not nervous or jumpy.
- ○ He is playful and shows a lively interest in his surroundings.

My test results:

exhibit confusion and behavioral changes. You can spare your dog this torment by having her spayed.

There are good reasons to neuter a male dog, too, especially if he displays exaggerated sexual behavior or is predisposed to develop testicular tumors.

Hormone therapy: The effect of regular hormone therapy on the female depends on how precisely it is carried out. Hormone administration should occur only during the resting part of the cycle (anestrus phase), which means at least three months after the end of the last heat cycle and no more than one month before the beginning of the next one. If the dog has an irregular cycle, her owner will not be able to pinpoint this period; only a vaginal smear per-formed by the veterinarian can deter-mine the timing accurately. It sometimes happens, though, that a female comes into heat despite the proper treatment. This can lead to the development of ovarian cysts, pyometra, and mammary tumors.

6

Training and Activities

Good training not only keeps your dog safe, it also allows her more freedom because then you can take her almost anywhere without problems. Dog-friendly activities foster her intelligence.

Early Training— Right From the Start

To make sure that the human-dog team functions smoothly right from the start, it is essential that you give your dog loving, consistent training. Take your time, and be patient.

More than 30 years ago, when I took my Collie puppy Tasso to a dog club in the hope that we would both learn something, I was advised to go back home and wait until the dog was a year old. Happily, thanks to Eberhard Trummler—at that time, he was the first behavioral scientist to write intelligible books about dog behavior—I was able to find my own way. Even today, though, many dog owners are still confused about when they should begin their dog's training.

The First Weeks of Life

As soon as the dog is born, life itself is his first teacher. The puppy learns instinctively to find his mother's milk supply, and until he leaves home, his mother gives him the first lessons in canine etiquette, like how to behave around higher-ranking dogs. She also is the first to set limits for him if he is too rough with her or his littermates (see photo, right). In addition, a good breeder makes sure the puppy is exposed to a variety of experiences during the first imprinting stage (see page 8). From the time you bring the puppy home, you are responsible for

his development and must pick up his education where his mother and the breeder left off. If you wait to train your dog until he is calling the shots, then it is too late.

In the brief period from the fourth until the sixteenth week of life, the puppy goes through the imprinting, socialization, and ranking stages. Everything that he learns, as well as everything he fails to learn, shapes his character. Lessons missed cannot be made up later.

This mother puts her puppy in his place with a muzzle grab. ▶

Choosing and Using the Right Leash

▶ **1** **10-foot (3-m) leash:** This is best for strolls around the block and little walks in high-traffic areas.

▶ **2** **30-foot (10-m) leash:** This leash, which can also be used as a long line, keeps the puppy safe in wide-open spaces and helps her learn to obey.

▶ **3** **6-foot (2-m) adjustable leash:** This leash can be shortened to 3 feet (1 m). It is ideal for training your puppy.

Training with Love and Understanding

Training a dog continues throughout her lifetime, because it must be geared to life with her human family. The first year of your growing puppy's training, in particular, entails a great deal of work and responsibility for you. It also demands a lot of your time and attention. It's your job to show the puppy what she may and may not do in all situations.

Personality: When training your puppy in an appropriate and humane way, you must never forget that she is a living creature who deserves to be treated with respect and whose unique personality you should try to understand. When you bring the puppy home, keep in mind that you are taking her away from the only family she has ever known. At first, she will be suffering from the shock of separation and feel lost and confused.

Although it's important to train the puppy to be compliant from the start, your goal should not be to have an automaton who simply follows orders, but rather a partner who enjoys living in harmony with her human pack members. Your task is to foster your dog's social intelligence and develop it through training.

Sense of achievement: Give your puppy a feeling of security by speaking to her authoritatively and consistently in clear, concise language (see Chapter 7). Your training must awaken your puppy's curiosity, challenge her in exciting ways, and motivate her by giving her a sense of achievement. This works best in everyday situations.

Dog school: It is wrong to believe that the dog will learn everything she needs to know in a "training course" that takes place once a week at a dog school. Nevertheless, it's a good idea to attend a course like this. It's not just the dog who's learning; you, as the dog's

owner, must acquire the knowledge necessary to train your puppy correctly. Unfortunately, many dog owners don't do anything with their pets outside of dog school. Training, though, must continue throughout the day; everything that goes into making a well-trained dog is best learned in situations that are part of the daily routine.

Constant supervision: Regardless of where you and your puppy are at the moment and what you are doing with her, all her actions require a consistent positive or negative reaction from you, or else you can simply ignore unwanted behavior.

The puppy's brain never stops learning, nor does she distinguish between free time and work. If there are times when you can't keep an eye on your puppy, put her in the crate for a little while (see page 43). It is important not to leave her unsupervised, because then she could do things that you don't want her to do (like gnaw on the

furniture, chew up shoes, or piddle in the house). Putting the dog in her crate temporarily is also good practice for when she has to stay alone. If you tire her out beforehand, then she will use the time in the crate to sleep. Puppies, like young children, still need a lot of rest.

TIP

Hold Treats the Right Way

There's a right way and a wrong way to hold food rewards. The right way: Hold the treat against the palm of your hand with your thumb and close the other fingers over it to make a fist. To reach the treat, the dog has to push your thumb aside with her nose.

When training the puppy, it is important that you **always use the same verbal signals.** Using different commands for the same thing confuses the dog.

How the Dog Learns

Your puppy gathers information from her environment, stores it in her memory, and retrieves the appropriate information in response to a specific stimulus; this is expressed as behavior.

Operant conditioning: When the puppy hears the stimulus word (verbal command) "Here," she comes to her owner and gets a reward for her behavior. She has successful/pleasant or unsuccessful/ unpleasant experiences. In this way, the puppy, like us, learns from experience. If we apply this principle skillfully when training her, then in the future the puppy will always

The puppy gets her favorite toy as a reward for the desired behavior.

be happy to repeat what she has experienced as pleasant and refrain from doing things that resulted in an unpleasant experience (like a sharp "No!" for instance, or being frightened by your shaking a can full of pennies). This learning principle is called operant conditioning.

Classical conditioning: Here a neutral stimulus triggers a specific behavior. For example, you get out the collar and leash. The dog is overjoyed at the prospect of a walk. She has learned by carefully observing and associating different invariable actions of her human that it's time for that walk she was hoping for.

Support measures: During the first 16 weeks, early exposure to new noises, smells, people, other kinds of animals, and machines fosters the development of the puppy's brain. Easy, playful exercises in the form of games, which she experiences as rewards, enhance her innate desire to learn. At no time in the future will your puppy be so teachable and so eager to learn as she is now. At the same time, the puppy is looking for a leader, one she can accept and to whose "benevolent" authority she can submit without reservation.

In all her actions, the puppy registers precisely how we respond to her behavior. If, in her opinion, we fail because of our inconsistency, lack of self-control, or unclear commands, then she cannot acknowledge us as "pack leader" (see page 33).

Building trust: A trusting bond between you and your puppy is the foundation for the puppy's smooth integration into the human-dog team. Clear rules make a human predictable for the puppy, give her a sense of security, and strengthen her trust. A dog trusts someone only when she is sure that nothing will happen to her when she's with that person. Likewise, if a puppy has complete trust in you as her owner, her reactions and behavior will always be predictable.

ignored by their pets and attempts at training go up in smoke.

Motivating your dog: A dialogue must take place between dog and owner, which requires the dog to concentrate on you and demonstrate her "willingness." To do this, it must be possible to motivate the dog, even as a puppy, at any time. Many factors are involved in achieving this. On the one

DID YOU KNOW THAT...

...dogs are usually happy to submit to us?

Dogs are adaptable and for this reason alone submit to people who behave in a consistent manner. Besides, they are egoists. Often enough with dogs, obeying commands depends on whether there's something in it for them. In this case, it doesn't matter to the dog if the person giving the commands is higher ranking or not. For dogs, a person is a sort of "top dog" with whom they have "adapted" to live according to the rules of a basic social order.

The bond between dog and human develops through regular physical contact, feeding, grooming, and doing things together outdoors. The more interesting you make different activities for you and your puppy, the more strongly she will bond with you. Then she'll scarcely let you out of her sight and it will be easy to get her attention during training. If a dog's bond with her owner is weak, though, almost anything else is more important to her. In this case, many dog owners are completely

hand, there are external stimuli such as treats, a lively game with you, or the encouraging tone of voice you use with the dog; on the other hand, internal stimuli, such as the puppy's curiosity, play a role. We distinguish between intrinsic motivation, which is based on internal stimuli, and extrinsic motivation, which is guided primarily by external stimuli. In order for you to be able to motivate your dog, though, the most important requirement is that you meet her basic needs. These include plenty of food and water, undisturbed sleep, security (practice in familiar surroundings), and a clear social structure in the human-dog team.

Getting Her Attention

Here's a practical example of how I get a puppy to focus on me: I use the phrase "Look, look!" to motivate the puppy to make eye contact with me, because the following exercise promises a tasty food reward.

Step 1: With the hungry puppy sitting in front of you, offer her a favorite treat. The moment she seizes the treat (not before and not after!), quickly say, "Look, look." Repeat this process at least five times.

Step 2: Next, wait until your dog becomes interested in something else nearby. Now, using the same tone of voice, say, "Look, look!" again several times. If the puppy responds quickly and shows her interest by making eye contact with you, she gets her treat.

Tip: The best place to practice this training exercise is in an area without any distractions. Using food to motivate the dog should eventually give way to self-motivation. To encourage this, always conclude the lesson on a positive note with the puppy's success. The sense of achievement is equivalent to an

1 **The command "Here!"** Squat down so you are at the puppy's level. Now motivate her to come to you by opening your arms wide and calling her in an encouraging tone of voice.

2 **"Here I am!"** Did your puppy rush over to you happily? Great! Now that she has done just what you wanted and sat down like a good dog, she naturally expects a reward.

The puppy waits attentively for ▶ a signal from her mistress.

intrinsic reward and later replaces the treat. Dogs trained using food alone, in other words with extrinsic motivation, expect greater and greater rewards as time goes by. Their motivation declines noticeably.

Basic Obedience

Obedience is the basis of good training, and it proves its worth in all situations later on. The puppy's obedience training is limited at first to the four most important concepts of her life, but she must master these perfectly: "Come," "Sit," "Down," and "No." For every family dog, these four key words are the foundation of a secure and harmonious life. From the time the puppy is about four or five months old, she is able to concentrate on learning these basic commands. You should, however, begin early training at eight to ten weeks of age. The puppy must learn the verbal signals and, after regular repetition, associate them with specific actions. Each time the puppy hears a specific signal, she will carry out precisely the action that she has associated with it. Always use the same verbal commands for the same actions! No dog will come reliably if you (or other family members) sometimes say "Come," sometimes "Here," and sometimes "To me." If you do that, she cannot associate the verbal command with the action. In addition, every dog, over the course of her life, learns a whole host of specific key stimuli

(words such as *walkies,* the names of her dog friends, and so on) by observing her human family. These can be positive stimuli or can benefit her in some way. They include sounds like the crinkling of a package of treats being opened or the sound of her owner's car.

Basic Commands

When learning the basic commands, the puppy must be on a leash so that she cannot run off if she is distracted. Use the lightweight 6-foot (2-m) puppy leash for this (see photo, page 94). The recall exercise can be practiced only in an area where there is absolutely no danger from traffic; here you can use the 30-foot (10-m) leash (see page 94).

MY PET

How Strong Is Your Puppy's Bond with You?

From time to time, it doesn't hurt to test the puppy's bond. Someone the puppy knows holds on to her while you hide behind a tree, a shrub, a fence, in a cornfield, or around the corner of the house as the dog watches.

The test begins:

○ First step: When you call to your puppy from your hiding place, your partner lets go of her so that she can look for you.

○ Second step: Same procedure, but this time don't call your puppy.

○ Third step: Make the hiding places increasingly difficult. Let your imagination run wild. The faster your dog wants to reach you, the stronger the bond.

My test results:

The "Come!" Command

Step 1: If, by chance, the puppy runs toward you excitedly because she wants to be with you, quickly squat down, open your arms wide to greet her, and motivate her to come to you by repeatedly saying "Come!" in a cheerful voice.

Step 2: Once the puppy reaches you, stroke her affectionately with both hands from head to tail and lavish praise on her.

Step 3: Conclude the exercise with a special treat as a reward.

Step 4: Later on, try motivating her to come to you in a wide-open area (with the 30-foot [10-m] leash) by

squatting down, calling her name, and saying "Look, look!" (see page 98). The moment she heads happily in your direction, call out "Come!" two or three times in an encouraging voice and conclude the exercise as described in Step 3. If, despite all your efforts to motivate her, the puppy hesitates or doesn't come at all, run away from her quickly. She'll be afraid of losing you and will try to follow you. If she runs after you, turn to her, squat down, and continue as described in Steps 1 to 3.

The "Sit!" Command

During the entire exercise, the puppy is on a loose leash.

Step 1: The puppy stands in front or to one side of you. Holding the treat, move it from the puppy's nose back over her head. Although she tries eagerly to reach the coveted treat, she doesn't get it until she shifts from this uncomfortable stance to the sitting position.

Step 2: As she sits down, say the verbal command "Sit!" Give her the treat the moment her bottom touches the ground.

Step 3: She must remain sitting while you praise her and stroke her from head to tail. After a few seconds, release her again with "Go on" or "Okay."

The "Down!" Command

For this exercise, your puppy must have mastered "Sit!"

Step 1: At the verbal command "Sit," the puppy sits down.

Step 2: Place one hand lightly on her rear end so that she can't stand up during the exercise. Holding a treat in front of her nose with the other hand, lower it to the ground while pulling it away from her so that she has to lie down in order to reach it.

Step 3: As soon as her belly touches the ground, say "Down!" and give her the treat. Praise her effusively and stroke her head and back gently with the hand you used to keep her from standing up.

The "No!" Command

A sharp "No!" should make the puppy immediately stop whatever she's doing, for example if she picks up something disgusting during a walk.

Step 1: If she has picked up something objectionable, walk toward her calmly,

take her by the collar, and say "No!" firmly without shouting. Give her collar a little tug as a correction, but don't be rough.

Step 2: As soon as she drops the object, praise her enthusiastically and give her a treat or her favorite toy in exchange.

Tip: Stay calm, because if you shout and storm over to the dog, you will succeed only in making her run off with her prize in an attempt to keep it safe. She'll think it's a game and try to get you to chase her.

"Sit!" is an easy command for the puppy to learn because, even as a youngster, she sat when she begged her mother for food.
▼

Advanced Puppy Training

Intelligent puppies learn best through play. You can help do your
part if you spend a lot of time with your puppy and find interesting games
to play with her. The result: a clever, even-tempered family dog.

Dogs have a natural need to play. Even puppies use their mother and siblings as playmates. Their games mainly involve chasing, fighting, and defending—but it's all in fun, never serious. This is how the puppies test their strength. The energetic rough-housing helps strengthen their body, especially their muscles, and the puppies gradually become aware of their physical capabilities. The innate mechanisms of social behavior are also tested, rehearsed, and reinforced through play.

Rules of the Game

When you bring your puppy home, there's nothing better to help her get over the loss of her mother, littermates, and familiar surroundings than playing with you. Right from the start, wise breeders try to foster their puppies' readiness to be motivated and learn by providing them with suitable toys and games. Dog and human get to know each other better by doing things together, and the bond of trust between the dog and her human playmate is strengthened. Even the dog's confidence increases. You, meanwhile, become acquainted with your puppy's body language and find out what she's like. As

you play, you'll be able to judge your dog's temperament and endurance, how tough or soft she is. Is she a bold adventurer or a sensitive soul? A family dog has to be cautious yet courageous, not a reckless daredevil. When you combine training and play, you can guide her behavior in the right direction.

Play is important: Only puppies who have had lots of opportunity to play with people become exceptionally playful, an attitude that often lasts a lifetime. Dogs with such well-developed play behavior are a pleasure to train when they are puppies as well as later on, when you can use games rather than force to continue their training. Dogs who quickly lose interest in playing obviously had too little opportunity to play when they were puppies. If a dog is reluctant to play, no matter how hard you try to motivate her later on, you'll meet with limited success.

No distractions: In the beginning, the puppy should not be distracted from the game. Start by playing indoors in familiar surroundings, where the puppy feels completely safe. Once the puppy begins to enjoy playing, you can gradually introduce little distractions by moving the game out into the yard and,

A piece of rope is great for developing physical strength and assertiveness.

later on, to someplace like a meadow away from your property. Once your puppy is used to playing where there are distractions, you can take her to a dog park to work with her.

Create a good mood: It is even more important, though, to create a trusting, friendly, and inviting atmosphere for the puppy when you play with her. The dog can sense your moods (see Chapter 7). If you're feeling grumpy, then it's better to take her for a walk until you're in a better frame of mind.

Set limits early: The first weeks in her new home are very turbulent for the puppy. Her curiosity drives her from one discovery to the next, and often she oversteps her bounds. It is your job to accompany her when she goes exploring, watching her and intervening when she overdoes it. So-called "play-

biting," for example, is very pronounced at first when the puppy roughhouses with humans. In this case, it is necessary to set limits for the puppy early in the game.

The dog has to master bite inhibition when she's just a puppy. If your puppy starts to bite, immediately stop the game with a loud "Ow!" Wait until the puppy lets go of your hand before you pull it away, though, and then distract her by throwing her a toy or a ball. If she accidentally bites your hand when she's playing, she must demonstrate bite inhibition by letting go immediately. If your puppy nips at your pants leg, get her back in line right away with a stern "No!" or grab her muzzle with one hand (see photo, page 119). Distract her by giving her a toy as a substitute.

You make the decisions: When playing with you, the dog must learn as quickly as possible that you are the

Playing with your puppy
fosters a strong bond
between the two of you.

one who initiates all games and that you determine when, what, where, how, and above all how long you play as well as which toys are used.

Puzzle toys are fascinating, even for a four-month-old puppy like this one.
▼

Playing with Other Dogs

After being separated from her littermates, your puppy should have the opportunity to attend a well-organized puppy kindergarten (at a dog club or dog school) once she has been adequately vaccinated. Here the puppy will be able to continue practicing social behavior and communication with other dogs.

Once they reach sexual maturity, most dogs have very few doggy friends they can play with comfortably. At some time or other they have had a bad experience because another dog refused to play with them. Dogs go through the same things we do. They don't take an immediate liking to every dog they meet. A male dog is not asocial when he fights with another dog. It's not important whether he fights, but rather how he fights and whether he observes the rules of social behavior when he does it so that nobody gets hurt—as long as people don't get involved.

Make Training a Game

At this point, I would like to return to our discussion of puppy training. For a dog who is socialized and trained using motivation and positive reinforcement rather than harsh treatment, almost everything she does with humans is a game.

Praise and the opportunity to satisfy her instincts continually spur her on so that she cheerfully carries out the tasks we set for her. I wish that people would stop trying to train dogs by demanding unconditional submission, as was once the case. Instead, they should use their knowledge of canine behavior to give

RECOMMENDED TOYS
FOR PUPPIES

HERE'S WHAT PUPPIES LOVE

Hard rubber ball or hard rubber ring	You can roll the ball or ring or throw it, and it's durable and easy to clean. Even a puppy has no trouble seizing the ring in her little mouth.
Prey dummy	This food-filled throw toy holds a tasty reward for the puppy when she successfully captures her "prey."
Floating dummy	A great toy for dogs who love to go swimming in the summer.
Sturdy knotted rope	Even old towels tied in knots can be used for playing tug-of-war with people or other dogs.
Squeaky toys	They often motivate dogs who are reluctant to play but can get on the owner's nerves.
Jute tug toys	Perfect for carrying around, throwing, or play-biting.
Boxes of different sizes	Great for hiding things for your puppy to find or simply for letting her tear apart.

the dog an opportunity to learn through play and carry out tasks happily and highly motivated.

Every Walk an Adventure

Nothing is more interesting for a dog than taking exciting walks with her human. How boring, then, if she is allowed out only in the yard to do her business. She already knows every tree, every bush, and every smell out there.

Add some excitement to your walks. In a park or an open field, you can use the 30-foot (10-m) leash. A popular game in dog circles is hide-and-seek, where you hide her favorite toy in the grass or shrubbery along the way. You could also discreetly drop your glove and then send your dog back to get it; for puppies, start with a distance of 1 to 2 yards (1–2 m) and gradually increase it. Or you could hide and have your puppy track you down. What the puppy wants to do most, though, is explore the area with you, catch leaves on the wind, sniff the unfamiliar odors, wander along the stream bank, climb over fallen trees or balance on the trunks, and investigate mouse holes. The puppy wants to experience the world in the

1 Ball games: Catching and carrying a ball is one of the classic play-hunting behaviors that puppies know without being taught.

2 Climbing up: It takes courage and agility to climb to the top of the ramp. It helps to put a few treats along the way.

3 Tunnel: In no time at all, any puppy will feel brave enough to run through this short tunnel. Later on, the tunnel can be lengthened.

safety of your company, but she doesn't want to be disturbed, followed, and interrupted incessantly as she explores because of your excessive solicitude. Intervene only when the puppy is really in danger.

If you stay near your puppy without speaking, she will always be aware of you. On the other hand, if you keep calling her, she has no reason to pay attention to you because she hears your voice constantly.

Tip: You can't take long walks with your puppy yet, but your outings should be interesting and motivating for her. If you meet other dogs, make sure they pose no threat before you allow your puppy to approach them.

Indoor Games

When you're indoors, you and the puppy can play without interruption, and you may even gradually teach a reluctant puppy to enjoy playing. Especially in bad weather, you should use every opportunity to keep the puppy busy.

Hiding treats: Start by hiding treats and then using the verbal command "Find!" Once she finds the treat, it's time for the next step. Hide her favorite toy, which you always indicate with the same name after the "Find" command, for instance "Find the bear!" or "Find the ball!" As the puppy gets older, you can take several toys that she knows by name and lay them in a circle, then have the dog fetch only the toy that you name.

Exercise course: You can create a little exercise course using ordinary household objects. It will be fun for your puppy while improving her physical fitness, testing her courage, and giving her some new things to experience. For example, make a weave course from filled plastic bottles and tempt her to go through it using treats and the command "Weave!" Lay an ironing board on stacks of books of different heights to make different "ramps" that challenge your puppy. You can also make marvelous tunnels and hiding places from sturdy boxes.

Rough-and-tumble play with you: Even a playful bit of roughhousing with you strengthens your puppy's feeling of belonging. In the process, the puppy learns how to handle physical contact trust. Avoid playing wild games on slippery floors. The puppy's ligaments and tendons are still developing, and they can be strained. Play with her only on a carpeted floor or a rug.

Interactive Dog Toys and Puzzles

You can now buy outstanding interactive toys for dogs. These include a number of highly recommended dog puzzle toys made of natural, untreated wood, which were developed by Swedish designer Nina Ottosson. Her interactive games stimulate the puppy's intelligence, foster an enjoyment of learning, and improve concentration. There are also imitation products on the market; make sure you check for the quality and safety of the materials used in them.

Of course, puppies still can't concentrate on solving the "problem" as long as older dogs, but nevertheless they are often surprisingly ingenious. Pushing wooden blocks around in order to get to a treat hidden beneath them is no problem at all for young canine geniuses.

Maze: Mazes can be assembled from ready-made pieces. Some dog clubs or schools use them for training. If you are good with your hands, you can build a little maze yourself. Perhaps you could use it to test your pet to find out how clever she is or how strongly she is bonded with you. The prerequisite is that your puppy obeys you even without a leash.

Have your dog sit at the start of the maze. You go to the other end and call your dog in a cheerful tone of voice. A puppy who ignores her owner will simply sit and wait. On the other hand, a strongly bonded puppy will look for the exit because she wants to reach her owner; motivated only by her owner's encouraging summons, this puppy will dash through the maze.

Partitions: The following simple experiment is also interesting. Stand behind a partition, for example a wooden divider or a folding screen, and have your puppy sit on the other side. Important: The puppy must be able to run behind the partition to find you. Now call the puppy. How does she respond? Does she try to come to you? How long does it take until she discovers that she can run around the partition by going right or left and finally reach you?

A Puppy as a Playmate

My son Tom is three years old. We just bought a puppy as a playmate for him. What should we keep in mind when the two are playing together?

Small children and puppies can be an explosive mixture. Under no circumstances should you let the two play together without supervision. Here you have two youngsters who are at about the same stage of intellectual development. Both child and puppy still react in completely unpredictable ways and must first get used to each other slowly. Furthermore, motor control in toddlers is still not fully developed. They often hold the puppy too tightly or drop her when they try to pick her up. Any painful experiences now could make the dog respond negatively to children in the future.

Foster Understanding

Right from the start, parents must explain to their child the proper way to treat the puppy and teach him to respect the dog as a living being. Above all, the child must learn not to treat the cute little puppy like a toy, but to be careful with her. The puppy must not be disturbed while she is sleeping, so the place where the dog sleeps is off-limits for children. The dog can retreat there when she wants some peace and quiet. Obviously, the puppy must not be disturbed when eating, either. Role-playing often helps make all of this comprehensible to a young child. Have your child play the part of a puppy who, for example, is being pinched by a child (played by you). Your child will quickly understand that it hurts. Also show your child how to recognize the puppy's warning signals and signs of displeasure, and explain why the puppy might not want to play just now.

Wild Games Are not Allowed

Do not allow your child to play wild games with the puppy that involve chasing, tugging, or biting. A puppy easily becomes overexcited when playing these games, and your child may feel the pain of her sharp little teeth. Children are usually not in a position to set serious limits for the puppy when roughhousing. All halfhearted attempts at defense are interpreted by the dog as further variations on the game, and she will become more and more wound up. In this case, an adult must intervene and, if necessary, remove the dog from the room until she calms down again. Frequent opportunities to romp with other dogs and participate in appropriate activities will let the puppy work off some of her excess energy and ensure that she is more even tempered.

Tip: In the beginning, don't make any of the tasks too difficult. The puppy must feel a sense of achievement with every game. Helping her without being obvious about it takes tact and sensitivity; after all, she should "earn" success by her own efforts.

Solitary Play

When a dog engages in playful activity by herself, experts call it solitary play. For example, this is what happens when young dogs have fun discovering their legs and how they move. They take delight in leaping into the air like baby goats, throwing themselves on the ground, and rolling around. When my French Bulldog Only was 12 weeks old, she discovered the garden pond with its partially submerged rocks, which she carefully proceeded to clamber up. When she had struggled to the top, she looked as proud as any mountain climber. To keep a dog entertained when she is alone, you can buy toys that can be filled with treats; when the dog rolls the toy across the floor, the treats fall out. Some dog owners think this is all they need to do to provide stimulation for their puppy. That's a big mistake, though!

Chewies: The most important solitary play activity for dogs of any age is gnawing and chewing on an object for hours. Make sure you provide plenty of safe, nontoxic chewies, such as branches, nonsplintering wood, rawhide, and cow's ears; otherwise the puppy may switch to chair legs or shoes.

Plush toys: Many dogs have a favorite plush toy, one they do not chew to bits. They usually carry this toy around for a long time and may even use it as a pillow when they sleep. Buy only special plush toys that are intended for dogs.

Tip: Toys that are used as motivational aids when training must be put away until the next lesson.

The puppy on the right is displaying the classic play-bow. Her playmate responds immediately with a raised tail, indicating that she is about to pounce. ▶

How Dogs Talk

The extent to which you can "converse" with your dog depends on how well you know his various "languages" and whether you understand how to interpret them correctly.

Dogs Speak
Several Languages

We humans have both a spoken language and a body language at our disposal. Dogs, on the other hand, can also communicate using an olfactory language and so-called "tactile" signals.

All canine behaviors associated with the communication between dogs and humans fall under the heading of expressive behavior. For dogs as well as humans, the ability to talk to each other (communication) is a prerequisite for harmonious coexistence.

Different Methods of Communication

We have a "narrative" language that lets us report what happened yesterday or describe what's on the agenda for tomorrow. The dog, however, uses an "indicative" language. He can communicate only what he is feeling or wants to express at the moment. And he "says" it using a wide variety of species-specific expressive behaviors. He "speaks" by means of
- movements of his body = visual signals,
- scents = olfactory signals,
- touch = tactile signals, and
- sounds = acoustic signals.

Dogs also use these modes of expression when they "talk" with us humans. After all, everyone is familiar with tail wagging, growling, and barking.

We humans communicate with each other using words, each of which has a specific meaning. We also have a body language, although in most cases we are able to use it only unconsciously. It plays a minor role in our social life. And yet it would be the easiest for our dogs to understand, because dogs are astute observers. Unfortunately, very few dog owners use body language to communicate with their four-legged friends.

You can even play when you're alone. ▶

Someone who knows how to interpret the body language of other people can tell, for example, whether a speaker is self-confident, insecure, or even lying. The conscious use of body language is something that can be learned in seminars and then applied in practice; for instance, it can help a person make a better impression in a job interview and thus get the job.

What the Dog's Body Language Tells Us

Even if you know nothing about the expressive behavior of dogs, you can immediately recognize that a dog is insecure or even afraid when he cowers in front of you with lowered head and tucked tail. Similarly, when a dog walks toward you with a stiff-legged gait, raised hackles, and bared teeth, it's clear that his intentions are not good. If he's friendly, though, he'll

DID YOU KNOW THAT...

...dogs don't need a sixth sense?

Sometimes our four-legged friends seem to have a sixth sense. They respond to our changing moods, can detect signs of disease, and warn us of impending disasters such as earthquakes. The dog is also able to alert a person to an oncoming epileptic seizure or a potentially fatal drop in blood sugar before the person is even aware of it. The explanation is simple: The dog smells it.

A dog can't lie. His body language always reveals what he honestly feels at the moment. His language is the language of feelings. The dog does not need words to express himself. He uses his entire range of vocalizations and body language as well as tactile and olfactory signals to communicate with other dogs and with us humans. It is important for us to know the dog's different modes of expression and to understand them correctly.

indicate it by giving you his paw or licking your hands.

Mind you, it is wrong to believe that a wagging tail by itself means a dog is friendly without paying attention to the rest of the dog's body signals. Only by looking at all the signs together—posture, ear position, facial expression, and tail carriage—can you tell what a dog's mood is at the moment. Our dogs have an extensive vocabulary, and they can combine the individual signals in various ways.

This allows the same signals to express a wide variety of meanings, depending on how they are combined.

The dog feels secure: An animal who feels completely secure in his environment displays neutral behavior by holding his head high, his legs relaxed and slightly bent, and his tail in the normal position for the breed. In dogs with erect ears, the ears are slightly turned toward the front; in dogs with hanging ears, the base of the ear is pulled forward.

The dog feels insecure: If the dog feels insecure, you can recognize that right away by his facial expression. The skin of the face is taut, and the corners of the mouth are pulled back. It looks as if the dog is trying to grin. His gaze is restless and not focused on anything in particular. The ears, or the base of hanging ears, are laid back. The head is down, the dog crouches, and the tail is tucked between the legs. Dogs display this behavior throughout life if they inherited a weak temperament from their parents or if they were socialized insufficiently or not at all during the imprinting period.

The dog postures: Self-assured male dogs sometimes engage in posturing when they meet a sexual rival. First, both dogs try to demonstrate their own superiority. They walk around each other with a stiff-legged gait. They hold their tails high and wave them slightly back and forth. They try to sniff each other's face or rear end, keeping head and muzzle level. However, any eye contact is strictly avoided. The ears are tilted slightly forward. One of the two can make defensive or aggressive threats, or else behave submissively. An

attack without advance warning is also possible.

Yet another expression of a confident dog is scraping the ground after urinating or defecating. The dog uses both hind legs or all four legs to do this. Marking

Mother is Boss

▶ **1** **Appeasement:** Both Belgian Tervuren puppies display submissive behavior toward their mother. The puppy on the left crouches, and the puppy on the right appeases by pawing.

▶ **2** **Submissive:** This puppy exhibits passive submission as well, this time by lying down and pawing in the direction of the mother's face (an appeasement gesture). Naturally, the mother responds affectionately to this behavior.

by males (females occasionally do it, too) is wolf-like behavior. It is used to demonstrate ownership of the territory. In urban areas, however, other males show little respect for this. Excessive marking leads to olfactory overstimulation, and the males keep on lifting their leg long after their bladder is empty.

Mounting, or at least hinting at mounting by placing a paw on another dog's back, should not generally be regarded as sexual behavior, but rather as an expression of dominance. Some males stand directly across the path of their rival in an assertive gesture, which is described as the T-position. All dominance behaviors are intended to demonstrate superiority and strength, but they also contain a veiled threat.

The dog threatens and attacks: Aggressive threats are also called offensive threats or aggressive threat behavior. In this behavior, always directed toward the opponent, the head is slightly lowered, the teeth are bared, and the lips are drawn back. The dog stares fixedly at his opponent. With ears laid back, the "attacker" growls or even barks. Because the dog stiffens his legs and raises his hackles (the hair on his shoulders and back), he appears larger. The tail is held high and stiff, depending on the breed. In wolves, the confrontation often ends at this point. In our domestic dogs, on the other hand, an attack can come immediately after this intimidation display, or it can even occur without any previous posturing. To some extent, dogs have forgotten how to fight without hurting each other.

The dog defends himself by threatening: In a defensive threat, the corners of the dog's mouth are drawn far back and the ears are flattened. The dog, who is usually feeling insecure, snaps spontaneously at the air; he crouches slightly, although his hackles may still be raised, and holds his tail tight against his belly. If possible, this dog will retreat, but if he cannot dodge his opponent or run away, he is ready to defend himself. Most dog bites are caused by "fear biters" like this. However, the defensive threat can also turn into passive submission.

The dog is submissive: In so-called passive submission, all eye contact is avoided and the dog shows no sign of aggression. The ears are laid back and the face has a puppyish look. The dog appears to be grinning, and he licks himself or just makes licking motions ("tongue flicking"). In the process, he may whine, whimper, cry, and even urinate. He lies on his back in the typical posture of a submissive dog. This strong signal triggers bite inhibition or kill inhibition when dogs are fighting or playing. With less intense body contact, the same inhibition can also be triggered when the submissive dog stands or sits and paws in the direction of another dog in an appeasement gesture, moving his front paw up and down. When he does this, the tail is tucked between his legs.

The dog submits voluntarily: In what is called active submission, the dog's trusting gaze is directed toward his partner, without staring, and his legs are bent so that he seems to be crouching. The tail is held low (not tucked between the legs) and wags back and forth rapidly. Active submission, in which the dog submits to a person

Body Signals
at a Glance

Trusting and "contrite" ▶

The Dachshund on the left exposes his belly trustingly to his owner. He wants a belly rub. The puppy on the right has apparently been reprimanded and is now showing that he is sorry.

◀ **Insecure and curious**

The laid-back ears of the puppy on the left indicate insecurity. The puppy on the right has perked up his floppy ears, and his expression indicates inquisitive anticipation. The facial expressions of dogs with furry faces can be difficult to interpret.

Calm and relaxed ▶
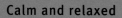

The "lip licking" in the photo on the left indicates a mood of calm and contentment. At the right, the puppy lies on his bed, completely relaxed, and looks up expectantly at his owner.

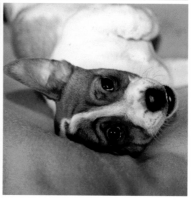

◀ *The puppy's crouching posture indicates active submission.*

dates back to puppyhood, when he would use this behavior to induce his mother to regurgitate predigested food for him.

The dog wants to play: There's no mistaking this invitation. The dog's front end almost touches the ground while his rear end is up in the air. The front legs are far apart, and the dog wags his tail. He may tilt his head or jerk it back and forth.

Vocalizations

Dogs can do more than just bark. Until they are four weeks old, you can hear them making contented sounds when they nurse.

Whining is a sound of distress that you hear in passive submission from puppies as well as adult dogs (see page 114). In active submission, the dog begs for attention by whining. In both cases, however, the whining can be replaced by barking, which is then combined with whimpering sounds. If passive submission is accompanied by extreme fear or pain, whining can escalate to yelping.

Puppies start to bark when they are four weeks old. A dog can express many different things by barking. Changes in pitch and the additional information conveyed by facial expression and body language in connection with a particular situation allow us to understand his barking over time.

or to another dog without being coerced, should be our dog's most common behavior. Unfortunately, because of the way many dog owners interact with their dogs every day, they force their dogs into a permanent state of passive submission, either through their own lack of self-control or by training the dog to obey blindly. In time, they turn their puppies into insecure, cringing, whimpering, urinating emotional cripples. Active submission, on the other hand, frequently merges into play behavior. My dog, for instance, shakes hands with me voluntarily and unrehearsed, licks my hands, or lies on his back in front of me so that I can scratch his belly. Sometimes he tries to lick my mouth. This "muzzle licking"

Growling is an expression of dominance as well as a threat. From the time they are eight weeks old, puppies will sometimes growl at a person to test their assertiveness. Growling is normal when dogs play with people.

When dogs are left alone for a long time, they howl. Howling is interrupted by frequent bouts of barking.

Scent Information

This so-called olfactory communication takes place, for example, when the dog leaves behind urine, feces, or the secretions of the anal glands. In this way, dogs can communicate with each other without actually coming face-to-face. Using scent marks that they deposit as urine and feces on places such as house corners, trees, or fence posts, dogs pass along information about themselves to other dogs. As a dog sniffs, he learns all sorts of details about the dogs who visited the spot before him and responds appropriately. A somewhat insecure dog will be intimidated by the scent of a dominant dog and will be careful not to defecate or urinate on this spot. On the other hand, in an animal of the same rank, this olfactory challenge triggers dominance behavior and is covered up with the dog's own scent mark. When two dogs meet, their sense of smell plays major role. They sniff each other's muzzle, genitals, and anus. This way they can recognize the other dog by smell if they have come across his scent marks before.

Puppies are ▶
naturally curious
and sniff at
everything they
come across. This
scent seems to
worry the puppy
a little, though.

The Art of Conversation

The dog is an astute observer, and he wants to please us humans. Your four-legged friend expects you to speak to him clearly, motivate him through praise, and make use of your body language. If you do this, you'll have no trouble communicating.

More and more of us find we have less and less time for personal conversations. Most chats take place over cell phones or computers. In contrast to face-to-face conversations involving eye contact, this type of communication makes it impossible as well as unnecessary to use our own body language or interpret that of the person we're talking to. In this way, the direct connection we had to each other is gradually slipping away. Unfortunately, the same holds true for communication with our dogs.

Speaking Clearly

To make sure you and your dog understand each other, your direct, personal presence, together with your body language, is of fundamental importance for your four-legged friend.

When you interact with your puppy, then, try to make clear use of your body language at the same time as your verbal language. Learn to interpret your puppy's body signals correctly by observing him carefully. In other words, learn the "vocabulary" of his language.

Dogs pay close attention to our body language. In this sense, the words that you use to give your dog individual commands are just a detail to make sure that he understands you correctly. The dog's reaction to our verbal signals also depends on the type of gestures we make, our posture, and even our facial expression.

Many people communicate only verbally with their dogs in a one-sided and peremptory manner: "Come!" "Sit!" "Down!" and so on. Even most training courses in dog schools are geared just toward having the dog learn to carry out these commands correctly. This is no basis for carrying on a lively conversation with your dog, though.

Then there are dog owners who confuse their pets with long-winded lectures and reprimands. The dog understands only the occasional word and eventually responds with complete indifference. He has absolutely no idea what his owner expects of him. At most, he senses that whatever he did, it annoyed his owner. Therefore, he uses his body language to indicate passive submission (see page 114), behavior that is often misinterpreted by his owner as a guilty conscience or even as shame. Dog owners like this should make a point of learning something about their dog's body language; otherwise the two will continue to have serious misunderstandings that interfere

While they are playing, the puppy's mother affectionately puts him in his place.

with any attempt at a harmonious life together.

Example: If you jabber away in an attempt to teach the puppy that you outrank him, he will not understand. However, he will catch on immediately if you put him in his place by grasping his muzzle, because he has already experienced the muzzle grab from his mother or from other adult dogs and understood what it meant (see photo, above). Don't wait to use this maneuver until your full-grown dog has become the boss in your family because you neglected something during his training. If you do, he will discipline you (!) very severely, biting you if necessary.

Verbal signals are important: Obviously, communication with the dog doesn't work unless we use our verbal signals. Even a puppy of average intelligence is able to learn 20 to 30 commands. Some specialists, such as good herding dogs or guide dogs for the blind, frequently master more than 100 different verbal signals. The dog is ready and able to understand what we say and comply with our wishes.

Human body language: Dogs are often far superior to us in interpreting our body language, something that often doesn't sit well with us. It's always amazing how quickly and intuitively dogs understand our body language, which is largely unconscious on our part. When we speak, there are many things we cannot control: facial expressions, gestures, tone of voice, pitch, or other peculiarities of the way we talk.

Signals to the Puppy

▶ **1** **Motivating:** When she squats down and opens her arms in a warm welcome, the puppy comes happily and without fear to his mistress.

▶ **2** **Threatening:** If you bend over a puppy like this, you will frighten him with your body language, which appears threatening to him.

▶ **3** **Ignoring:** If you don't like having a friendly puppy jump up on you, you must turn away abruptly from the dog and simply ignore him.

Yet even a puppy can tell what kind of a mood his owner is in at the moment, because after thousands of years of coexistence, the dog has obviously developed a special kind of intelligence to understand us humans better.

Be Ready to Communicate

At first, the most you can expect of a puppy is that he comes to you quickly on command and responds to praise and criticism as desired. The prerequisite for communication between you and your dog, though, is a "readiness to communicate."

Puppies are, by nature, always ready to communicate with us. Of course, you have to recognize his readiness and reinforce it. If you respond negatively to your dog's attempt at communication, you will nip it in the bud.

Errors in communication also hinder the "conversation." These include, for example, unclear instructions to the dog, attempts at help that confuse him, or poor timing when he's learning something.

A good example: Your puppy should come to you quickly and reliably. Here's how to make it easy.

Step 1: He needs a clear and distinct command from you: "Come!" When you do this, squat down so that you don't intimidate him by towering over him.

Step 2: Now give the visual cue, which is always the same: Open your arms wide, with your palms turned upward. Beckon to him with your fingers. Your body language now tells the puppy clearly that you welcome him. Because he knows from experience that he sometimes gets a reward and lots of petting for coming, he will certainly not run past you.

Corrections

Correcting the dog has nothing to do with punishment. There is no need for punishment in training based on positive reinforcement. A dog who is punished after the fact for doing something wrong learns absolutely nothing, because the punishment just causes him stress. Furthermore, the puppy's readiness to communicate is disrupted by the punishment. This is why the correction must be given as soon as the dog makes a mistake. Try to get into the habit of producing a deep, growly "No!" If you can really growl threateningly, then you can do away with your verbal "No!" Your dog just has to sense it as a negative signal. This signal alone isn't enough, though. All you've done is let him know that what he just did is wrong. This negative experience must always be followed by a positive alternative for the dog. Help your dog to do everything correctly, and give him positive reinforcement when

he has succeeded with your help. In the future, he will always be more attentive (ready to communicate), because he is interested in performing the assigned task to your satisfaction. With a dog like this who is ready to communicate, it is possible to be increasingly gentle when making a correction.

Tip: I keep the puppy on a leash for all stages of his education and training. The length of the leash depends on

TIP

The Dog Does Not React Normally

Usually this is the result of neuroses that can develop during puppyhood because of inadequate socialization and/or serious training errors. Health problems such as back pain, hip pain, or headaches caused by a brain tumor can also be responsible.

▲

*This posture is an invitation
to play.*

where you are training or which exercise you are working on (see pages 94–95). The dog has to earn the right to go without a leash during a lesson by demonstrating that he responds to correction and is reliable.

Punishment is taboo: Time and again you hear dog owners talk about so-called natural punishments. Shaking the dog by the scruff of the neck is supposedly something even mother dogs do with their pups. In the wild, this scruff-shake equates with "killing" and can, when used as a punishment, terrify a puppy. No mother dog would do that to her puppies.

I also disapprove of the advice to pinch or twist the dog's ear, because this can injure the ear; besides, I regard dog training as a partnership between me and the dog, so inflicting pain is

out of the question. I'll refrain from listing any more supposedly natural methods of punishment, because I believe that using punishment as a means of correction, which happens in many training facilities even today, should have no place in modern dog training. The dog learns nothing by being punished, because it happens after he has already done something wrong. Use foresight when training your dog so that he cannot make any mistakes.

Gentle and Friendly

Never yell when giving verbal commands. The louder you get, the less attentive your dog will be, because your volume doesn't motivate him to pay attention. Verbal commands must be clear and distinct, yet spoken in a soft and friendly voice. The power of your voice alone will not make your dog more obedient. You will hold your puppy's attention better if you speak to him softly. Shouting is unnecessary, especially since a dog hears far better than we do. Your four-legged friend simply asks that you speak clearly and distinctly at a normal volume and use the appropriate body language.

When my seven-year-old German Shepherd Dog Itchy corrects our 13-week-old French Bulldog Only, the older dog generally uses eye contact and, at most, wrinkles her nose and growls softly. In the first weeks, the corrections were undoubtedly a bit more intense and direct, but they never involved force, angry outbursts, or the infliction of pain.

Praising Correctly

Praise serves as positive reinforcement for the puppy's desirable behavior. Correction only lets him know what he has done wrong (see page 121).

I am frequently amazed at what some people think it means to praise their dog. Some pat him vigorously on the head or "smack" him appreciatively on the ribs, others just mutter an unenthusiastic "good dog," and still others hand out treats indiscriminately at every opportunity. But dogs don't know what to make of "praise" like this, to say nothing of associating it with their good behavior. Praise plays a central role in communication between human and dog. What I mean by this is quietly and affectionately stroking the dog while voicing your approval. Never be stinting with praise, but always use it for a purpose, otherwise it will lose its effectiveness.

Praise is the key to success. Your puppy understands you best when you reward every small step of an exercise rather than waiting until he has completed the entire exercise. Correct praise must reinforce whatever the dog is doing at the moment and motivate him to keep going. He must regard praise as something positive and associate it with whatever action you find desirable. Praise is an intense form of communication. That's why your cheerful tone of voice and positive body language must match the praise and be "genuine." The dog notices right away if you are praising him only perfunctorily or are overdoing it.

Eye to Eye

Eye contact is important not only in communication between people, but also in dealing with a dog. An attentive dog who is ready and willing to communicate is looking for relaxed eye contact with his owner. He displays active submission (see page 116). On the other hand, he will regard a fixed stare (direct, hard eye contact) as a threat and a challenge. A dominant

The puppy jumps from a crouch into a play-bow, hoping someone will join the fun.
▼

◀ *This patient German Shepherd puppy looks at his owner expectantly because he is hoping for a lively romp.*

dog could respond by attacking. Let's assume your puppy oversteps his bounds when you're playing with him and you have a hard time getting him under control again. In this case, as well as in other circumstances where you have to set limits for him, it helps to "read him the riot act": Grasp your dog's head gently in both hands and try to maintain eye contact without glaring at him. Speak to him quietly and say very emphatically "Stop that!" When you do this, don't shake the dog's head back and forth or yell. You'll be surprised at how your composure and firmness are communicated to the dog. After you "dismiss" the dog, ignore him until he makes another attempt at communication, at which point you must respond by giving him something else to do.

Appeasement Gestures

Dogs use gestures that inhibit aggression and pacify their opponent.

This works perfectly with other dogs. However, these signals are usually misinterpreted by dog owners.

Yawning: The dog uses this to calm an aggressive adversary. His behavior counteracts a threat or an attack.

Scratching himself: This is used often and effectively in encounters between dogs to pacify an aggressive opponent. The dog who scratches himself must, however, be the more confident one, because a weaker dog doesn't have the "nerve" to sit down and scratch in the presence of a threatening adversary when he doesn't have an itch.

Sniffing: You frequently see this behavior at dog parks in conjunction with dog handlers who are excited or out of control. The dog's sniffing indicates that he's had some bad experiences after coming when his handler called. The dog approaches hesitantly because he can already tell from the handler's body language that he is irritated. A dog who has been taught to heel using force or harsh corrections (hard tugs on the leash with a choke chain or a prong collar) will also sniff as he runs along in front of or next to his handler in order to pacify him. In this way, the dog hopes to prevent the person from inflicting further pain on him.

Licking: The puppy still remembers this behavior from when he licked his mother's mouth to beg for food (see "muzzle licking," page 116). Now he repeatedly licks his muzzle or just flicks his tongue when he feels intimidated or threatened.

Shaking hands: When the dog displays this behavior, many people believe that he's trying to say hello. Actually, this is a classic appeasement gesture and is understood as such by other dogs. In this very cautious signal, the lower-ranking dog sometimes even touches his threatening adversary with an outstretched paw without ever being bitten. If the subordinate dog were to place his paw on the other dog's shoulder or touch the other dog's face with it, it could be interpreted as a provocation.

MY PET

How Often Does Your Puppy Make Appeasement Gestures?

In order to improve communication between you and your dog, you should learn to recognize and interpret the appeasement gestures that he uses with you or with other dogs.

The test begins:

○ Pay closer attention to the body language your puppy uses with you as you go about your daily activities together.

○ Make a note of his appeasement gestures (see page 124) and the circumstances under which he uses them. If he is excessively submissive, think about what you could have done wrong in a particular situation to make him want to appease you.

My test results:

Questions About Communication

? **On Sunday mornings—but only then—my dog sits eagerly at the front door because that's the day we take him to the puppy playground. How does he know when it's Sunday?**

Quite simple: Your dog notices it because your routine is different that day. Maybe you sleep longer on Sundays, everybody has a pleasant breakfast together, and you put on special clothes for training the dog. Your dog obviously seems to enjoy these outings; otherwise he would not look forward to them.

? **Can dogs feel ashamed?**

No, even though it sometimes looks that way when we correct the dog for making a mistake. Then, depending on how sensitive he is, he responds more or less strongly to our displeasure and shows all the signs of submission. Shame would presuppose

a moral consciousness. Dogs have no concept of right and wrong and consequently no guilty conscience. They do not act according to the principles of good and evil, but rather follow their instincts (see page 13).

? **Our four-month-old German Shepherd mix is afraid of traffic, although he has had no negative experiences because he grew up on an isolated farm.**

The puppy apparently never had an opportunity to get used to traffic in the quiet environment where he was born. Gradually familiarize him with traffic in a relatively untraveled area or at a time when traffic is light. Always practice on the same quiet street until he has become used to cars in these familiar surroundings. If the puppy seems to be afraid, you should not comfort him; just act nonchalant and pay

no attention to his fear. If you tend to be anxious and nervous, don't attempt to train him yourself. The dog can read your mood, and sensing your insecurity will make his condition worse.

? **How can I recognize and interpret my dog's facial expression?**

Even we humans can understand a dog's body language fairly well. On the other hand, we often have trouble correctly interpreting facial expressions—the rapid changes in eyes, lips, eyebrows, or forehead wrinkles—which must be evaluated along with posture and tail carriage. Furthermore, it's almost impossible to make out facial expressions in some breeds with heavily furred faces.

So here's my tip: Study your dog's facial expressions in different situations by making sketches of him.

You'll be amazed at how many interesting things you'll learn about your dog.

? My four-month-old Smooth Fox Terrier often raises his hackles when he meets other dogs. Does he have aggressive tendencies?

First of all, this behavior is a sign of stress. Even with us, terror can literally make our hair stand on end. If the dog is only slightly upset but still confident, he will raise just the hair on his shoulders. On the other hand, if he feels more agitated, insecure, and anxious, the hair all along his back will stand on end. The trigger in all cases is the stress hormone adrenaline. Puppies sometimes simply experiment with this starting at about 10 weeks of age. Make sure your puppy has increased regular contact with socially well-adjusted dogs.

? Why doesn't our puppy scrape the ground after he does his business? All the dogs in our neighborhood do it.

Your neighborhood dogs are no doubt sexually mature adults. Dogs don't scratch in the dirt like cats to bury their feces. On the contrary, dogs do it to spread around the scent mark they leave when they deposit urine or feces. Dogs have sweat glands on their feet that transfer their individual scent to the ground when they scratch. In addition, scraping the ground intensifies the scent mark. Once your puppy reaches puberty, he will behave just like your neighbors' dogs. Females, by the way, mark and scratch less often than males.

? What is the best way to introduce my dog to an unfamiliar dog?

Even if the two dogs are still puppies, their first meeting should take place on neutral territory, for example in a big meadow. Here they both have plenty of room to get acquainted by playing. Even puppies become territorial in their own homes and may try to defend their property. Once the two dogs have become friends, disputes will rarely arise in each other's homes. Make sure, though, that your own dog has more rights in "his" home. His favorite toy should be kept out of reach of the other dog.

What to Do When There Are Problems

Sometimes the human-dog relationship can experience problems or simply misunderstandings. Although they can have many different causes, they are usually easy to remedy.

Minor Problems and Their Solutions

Here you'll find an assortment of canine behaviors that we humans find annoying. It's not terribly difficult, though, to arrive at some common ground with the dog.

Even the best dog can sometimes exhibit unwanted behavior. You might laugh off some of your pet's idiosyncrasies, but sometimes enough is enough. Before you start trying to retrain her, though, first attempt to find the reason for her behavior and eliminate it. For example, if you are trying to break your male dog's habit of chasing everything he sees or fighting with other male dogs, you usually won't achieve any lasting success, because this is part of normal canine behavior. Ultimately, the only thing that will help here is to keep the dog on a leash. With dangerous habits like fear-biting or attacking people, you definitely need the help of an experienced animal behaviorist.

Chasing Cars or Bicycles

Chasing anything that moves is part of a dog's natural behavior. It is innate (see Those Wonderful Instincts, page 13). The dog is a "coursing predator" who hunts by pursuing her prey, so her eyes are extremely sensitive to movement. She can spot the slightest motion. Even young dogs love to chase wind-blown leaves, butterflies, or scraps of paper. As they get older, dogs like this will develop an interest in chasing bicycles or even cars, especially if they are given more freedom than their obedience warrants.

Possible solutions: Even in puppyhood, you must prevent your leashed dog from any independent attempt at chasing things (even leaves), especially in high-traffic areas. If your dog is crazy about chasing, you should start training her early on to retrieve or carry suitable objects. If she is already chasing cars or bicycles, she must be

Lively and high-spirited, this puppy races through the grass. Hopefully she hasn't spotted any "prey."

Puppy Behavior

▶ **1** **High spirits:** If a puppy gets carried away when playing, she may snap at your hand with her sharp little teeth. You should discourage this right from the start.

▶ **2** **Left alone:** Puppies show fear of abandonment by howling interspersed with barking.

▶ **3** **Submissive:** A large, unfamiliar dog triggers passive submission in puppies. In some cases, this behavior can be lifesaving.

kept on a leash at all times. If she starts to chase something, abruptly change directions. If she allows you to distract her this way, praise her extravagantly. At the same time, devote more attention to obedience training.

Chewing on Things

Puppies aren't the only ones who enjoy chewing on all sorts of objects, including furniture and valuable carpets. Dogs find shoes especially interesting, either because they smell like leather or because they bear the scent of a beloved person. Some dogs chew only when they are teething, whereas for others it's a lifelong habit.

Dogs frequently chew up things because they are bored, afraid, lonely, or have an excess of energy.

Possible solutions: Put away any prized possessions that could tempt

your dog to nibble. Keep her supplied with new chewies, for example a cow's ear, a piece of rawhide, old cardboard boxes, empty milk cartons, a length of old rope, or an old broom. If she still goes for chair legs or other parts of the furniture, coat them with hot pepper sauce or bitter apple. Dogs really dislike that. Continue to keep a close eye on your pet, though, to make sure she doesn't look for new things to chew.

Jumping Up

Jumping up is an innate canine greeting ritual. A dog that jumps up on us exuberantly is exhibiting perfectly natural behavior, even if we don't appreciate it, and should not be punished for it. Ignore the outmoded advice to knee the dog painfully or step on her hind foot when she jumps up.

Possible solutions: In the future, insist that the dog sit for every greeting. Only then do you pet her and occasionally reward her with a treat. If she attempts to jump up, fend her off with a sharp "No!" and abruptly turn away. Greet her only after she sits at your signal. Also ask your friends not to greet your dog or pay attention to her until she sits.

Digging Holes

When an energetic dog with too little to do spends any length of time in the yard without supervision, she often fights boredom by digging large holes. Maybe the dog just enjoys this activity, or maybe she has watched you "hide" tulip bulbs and is trying to imitate you.

Possible solutions: Even when your dog is just a puppy, put an end to this sort of activity right away. Don't

allow her to dig during walks, either. Otherwise, she won't understand why she's not allowed to do it at home. Spend more time with your dog so that she doesn't get bored. Do not leave her in the yard without supervision. A sharp "No!" can prevent her from digging only if you are there. If she

TIP

Fear of Other Dogs

You and your "scaredy-cat" should take walks with other dog owners and their "brave" dogs. Try to find out the distance at which your dog shows no fear of another dog. Gradually decrease this distance. Reward your dog whenever she behaves in a relaxed manner.

You should correct undesirable behavior **during puppyhood**. Then your life together will be much more harmonious later on.

always digs in the same spot, put some of her own (!) feces in the hole and cover it up again lightly with dirt.

Separation Anxiety

Dogs suffering from separation anxiety bark, howl, or whine, often for hours at a time; some even destroy the furniture. Separation anxiety can be attributed to various causes. Often these dogs have lost a significant person once before. Just as frequently, though, this anxiety occurs in dogs who have never been left alone because their owner is usually home all day.

Possible solutions: Step-by-step, help the dog feel more secure by training her

that you are indeed coming back. First, it is important to tire her out. Then take her to wherever she sleeps. If she lies down, leave the room—without speaking—and close the door. After no more than five seconds, come back again, but don't speak to the dog. You must get her used to your frequent comings and goings. Occasionally you can even take your coat and quietly leave the house. Don't stay away too long, though.

Dispense with any ceremony when you leave or come back. The dog must regard the departure and return of her special person as the most natural thing in the world. Once she is used to it, gradually prolong your absence by a few minutes each time.

When puppies grow up with cats, it's not unusual for true friendships to develop.

▼

Fear of Thunderstorms and Fireworks

During a thunderstorm, dogs sense the electrical charge that's in the air and produces lightning and thunder. Dogs recognize the power of nature in all this and want to seek shelter from it. Dogs who are anxious and somewhat insecure suffer more from a severe thunderstorm, but even for dogs with nerves of steel it is often scary—they just don't panic right away. Fireworks trigger the same feelings in nervous dogs as thunderstorms do. These dogs are usually not "steady" to the sound of gunshot, either, and are especially sensitive to noise.

Possible solutions: Stay indoors and close the windows and blinds so that the dog can't see the lightning or rockets and so that the thunder or noise of the fireworks is muffled. Put on some music, instead, and turn up the volume a bit louder than usual. Never console the frightened dog or coddle her. That will only make her think she's right to be afraid. Act completely unconcerned and perhaps

Rolling in Smelly Stuff and Eating Feces

Rolling in disgusting things is a behavior our dogs have inherited from their ancestor, the wolf.

Wolves concealed their predator's scent by rolling in the droppings of herbivores when they went hunting.

DID YOU KNOW THAT...

...some problems require an expert?

With serious behavioral problems, such as aggression toward people, you have to seek the advice of an expert. A good animal behaviorist will evaluate not just the dog but the behavior of the owner as well. During the consultation, the behaviorist will first determine what's causing problems for both dog and owner and then recommend a course of treatment. Trying to discover the underlying reasons for the behavior always takes up most of the visit.

try to distract your dog with a game. There are also mild tranquilizers for dogs (consult your veterinarian).

Alternatively, you can try to get your dog used to the sound of thunderstorms. Make a recording of the thunder and play it back for her while she's eating. Do it so softly at first that she shows no sign of nervousness. Increase the volume slowly day by day. The next time there's a thunderstorm, feed your dog just as you did when you were training her with the recording.

Our dogs prefer to do it just after they've had a bath. Apparently, their idea of what smells good is completely different from ours.

Eating feces can be caused by a variety of factors. Frequently an unbalanced diet is to blame, because the dog's food may lack alkaline ingredients that she, as a scavenger, absolutely must have. A deficiency in certain minerals is also possible. It can be, though, that your dog feels neglected.

MY PET

Why Isn't It Working?

For most problems and misunderstandings that arise when living with a dog, the animal bears absolutely none of the blame. Maybe you gave your dog the wrong signals or misinterpreted her behavior. Try to get to the bottom of it.

The test begins:

Does your puppy recognize that you're the boss (see page 33)? Does she have absolute trust in you? Does she feel secure in your presence? Could she be sick? Have you motivated the puppy enough? Was she focused on you and attentive? What was distracting her? Were your commands clear? Could you have expected too much of her with this exercise, perhaps by skipping steps in the training?

My test results:

Possible solutions: If your dog has a penchant for rolling in excrement, the only things that will help are your vigilance and your dog's obedience. She must immediately stop what she's doing at a sharp "No!" or "Yuck!" from you.

In order to counteract feces-eating (coprophagy), first clean up all the dog droppings in the yard. When you take your dog out for a walk, keep her on a leash so that you can intervene right away to prevent her from eating feces.

Have your veterinarian determine whether your dog is suffering from a nutritional deficiency; if it turns out that this is the case, think about changing your dog's food and feeding her a natural diet (fresh meat) in the future. In Chapter 4 of this manual, I give you detailed recommendations on how to do this. I can guarantee you that animals who are fed fresh foods do not eat feces.

"I'm doing great!" You can tell that just ▶
by looking at this little Siberian Husky.

Pet Sitter's Checklist

Sometimes you can't take your dog with you. Maybe you have to go to the hospital, or you want take a trip by yourself and a pet sitter will be looking after the dog for a while. Here's a place for you to write down everything a temporary caregiver should know. This way, your four-legged friend will be in good hands while you're away.

My dog's name:

This is what he/she looks like:

This is what he/she likes to eat:

This amount every day:

This amount once a week:

Occasional treats:

This is what he/she drinks:

Feeding times:

This is where the food is kept:

Housekeeping:

This is cleaned every day:

This is cleaned once a week:

This is how he/she likes to be petted:

Great activities for him/her:

He/she really dislikes this:

Things my dog is not allowed to do:

This is also important:

The dog's veterinarian:

You can reach me here:

INDEX

The page numbers in **bold** type refer to illustrations.

Associations and Clubs

American Kennel Club (AKC)
8051 Arco Corporate Drive,
Suite 100
Raleigh, NC 27617-3390
Tel.: (919) 233-9767
www.akc.org

**American Rare Breed
Association (ARBA)**
9921 Frank Tippett Road
Cheltenham, MD 20623
Tel.: (301) 868-5718
www.arba.org

Canadian Kennel Club (CKC)
200 Ronson Drive, Suite 400
Etobicoke, Ontario M9W
5Z9, Canada
Tel.: (416) 675-5511
www.ckc.ca

**German Kennel Club
(*Verband für das Deutsche
Hundewesen, VDH*)**
Westfalendamm 174
44141 Dortmund, Germany
www.vdh.de

The Kennel Club (KC)
1-5 Clarges Street
Picadilly, London W1J 8AB
United Kingdom
www.thekennelclub.org.uk

**North American Mixed Breed
Registry (NAMBR)**
21 Trapnell Street
St. Catherines, Ontario L2R
1B, Canada
www.nambr.ca

United Kennel Club (UKC)
100 E. Kilgore Road
Kalamazoo, MI 49002-5584
Tel.: (269) 343-9020
www.ukcdogs.com

**World Canine Organization
(*Fédération Cynologique
Internationale, FCI*)**
Place Albert 1er, 13
B-6530 Thuin, Belgium
www.fci.be

USEFUL WEBSITES

BARF Diet

BARFWorld
www.barfworld.com

Health Care

**AltVedMed (Complementary
and Alternative Veterinary
Medicine**
www.altvetmed.org

**American Veterinary Medical
Association**
www.avma.org

**Free Animal Health
Resources from the College
of Veterinary Medicine at
Cornell University**
www.vet.cornell.edu/library/
freeresources.htm

**Healthy Pet (American
Animal Hospital Association)**
www.healthypet.com

**The Merck Veterinary
Manual Online**
www.merckvetmanual.com

**Pet Health Care (Doctors
Foster and Smith)**
www.peteducation.com

Veterinary Partner
www.veterinarypartner.com

Insurance

**"Pet Insurance" (American
Animal Hospital Association)**
www.healthypet.com/PetCare
/PetInsurance.aspx

Pet Sitters

**National Association of
Professional Pet Sitters**
www.petsitters.org

Pet Sitters International
www.petsit.com

Poisonous Plants

**"Plants Poisonous to
Livestock" (Cornell
University Department of
Animal Science)**
www.ansci.cornell.edu/plants

"Toxic and Non-Toxic Plants"
www.aspca.org/pet-care/
poison-control/plants

Books for Additional Information

American Kennel Club. *The
American Kennel Club Dog
Care and Training,* 2nd ed.
New York: Wiley Publishing,
2002.

Birmelin, Immanuel. *How
Dogs Think: A Guide to a
Beautiful Relationship.* New
York: Sterling Publishing,
2007.

Burch, Mary R., and Jon S. Bailey. *How Dogs Learn.* New York: Howell Book House, 1999.

Coren, Stanley. *The Intelligence of Dogs.* New York: Free Press, 2005.

Coren, Stanley, and Sarah Hodgson. *Understanding Your Dog for Dummies.* Hoboken, NJ: Wiley Publishing, 2007.

Fogle, Bruce. *The New Encyclopedia of Dog Breeds.* New York: Dorling Kindersley Publishing, 2000.

Hegewald-Kawich, Horst. *Dogs from A to Z* (Compass Guides). Hauppauge, NY: Barron's Educational Series, 2005.

Kahn, Cynthia (ed.). *The Merck/Merial Manual for Pet Health (Home Edition).* Whitehouse Station, NJ: Merck & Co., 2007.

Ludwig, Gerd. *Practical Handbook: Dogs.* Hauppauge, NY: Barron's Educational Series, 2005.

Schlegl-Kofler, Katharina. *The Complete Guide to Dog Training.* Hauppauge, NY: Barron's Educational Series, 2006.

Schmidt-Röger, Heike. *300 Questions About Dogs* (Compass Guides). Hauppauge, NY: Barron's Educational Series, 2006.

Wolf, Kirsten. *Games and Sports for Dogs.* Hauppauge, NY: Barron's Educational Series, 2010.

Magazines

AKC Gazette
American Kennel Club
(800) 533-7323
www.akc.org

AKC Family Dog
American Kennel Club
(800) 490-5675
www.akc.org

Dog Watch
P.O. Box 420235
Palm Coast, FL 32142-0235
(800) 829-5574

FCI Magazine
(In English, French, German, and Spanish)
www.fci.be/magazine.aspx

Acknowledgments

My wife, Hansi, deserves special thanks. Not only has she shown tremendous understanding for my many dog-related activities over the past 45 years, but she has also been unfailingly patient, even when I was sometimes preoccupied with writing my books.

Author and publisher thank the firm of Padvital GmbH, Karlsfeld, Germany, www.padvital.de, for Swedish designer Nina Ottosson's dog puzzle toys, which are shown in the photos.

Important Information

The recommendations in this manual apply to normally developed puppies from good stock—in other words, healthy animals with no character flaws. If you adopt an adult dog, you must realize that he has already been influenced significantly by his experiences with other people. You should observe the dog carefully, including how he behaves toward people. You should also have a look at the previous owner. If the dog is from an animal shelter, the staff there may be able to tell you something about the dog's history and idiosyncrasies. Some dogs, because of bad experiences with people, behave abnormally and may also have a tendency to bite. These dogs should be adopted only by experienced dog owners. Even with dogs who are well trained and carefully supervised, there is always a chance that they will damage somebody's property or even cause accidents. It is always advisable to make sure you have adequate insurance coverage.

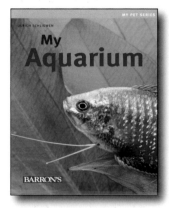
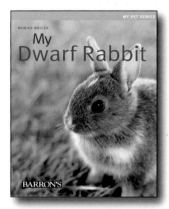
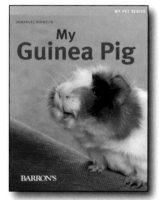
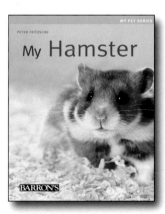
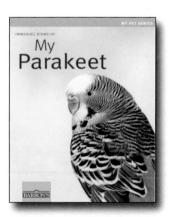

Picture Credits

Arco-Digital: 18–2, 19–3;
Debra Bardowicks: 48, 49–1, 49–2, 79–1, 79–2;
Thomas Brodmann: 94, 95–1, 95–2, 101, 104, 105, 106–1, 106–2, 106–3, 120, 121–1, 121–2, 130, 131–2, C7;
Seth Casteel: 20–2, 22–1;
Corbis: 34, 108;
Oliver Giel: 7, 16–2, 17–2, 36, 39–1, 39–2, 51, 54, 68, 69–1, 69–2, 73, 75, 77–1, 77–2, 77–3, 77–4, 85–1, 85–2, 85–3, 87, 89–1, 89–2, 93, 96, 119, C8;
Juniors: 20–3, 22–3, 23–1;
Liz Kaye: 27–3;
Angela Kraft: 2–2, 15, 23–2, 31, 32, 102, 124;
Regina Kuhn: C1/Cover, 44, 47, 59–1, 59–2, 59–3, 67, C4–1;

PantherMedia: 20–4;
Pets by Paulette: 22–2;
Sigrid Starick: 17–3, 19–2, 24–3, 26–2, 26–3;
Christine Steimer: 4, 11, 16–1, 18–1, 19–1, 20–1, 21–1, 21–3, 23–3, 25–1, 25–3, 27–2, 29, 38, 41–1, 41–2, 41–3, 41–4, 41–5, 41–6, 52, 56, 64, 71, 81, 82, 86, 98–1, 98–2, 127–1, 127–2, 127–3, 129, 132, C3–1;
Tierfotoagentur: 17–4, 21–2, 24–1, 24–2, 25–2, 25–4, 26–1, 27–1;
Monika Wegler: 2–1, 3, 5–1, 5-2, 6, 8–1, 8–2, 9, 10, 12, 14, 17–1, 18–3, 30, 35, 37, 40, 43, 45, 50, 53, 60, 61, 63, 65, 66, 74, 78, 83, 88, 90, 92, 97, 99, 103, 109, 110, 111, 112, 113–1, 113–2, 115–1, 115–2, 115–3, 115–4, 115–5, 115–6, 116, 117, 118, 122, 123, 128, 131–1, 133, 135, 145, C2–1, C2–2, C3–2, C3–3, C4–2, C4–3, C4–4, C5–1, C5–2, C6–1, C6–2.

All inquiries should be addressed to:
Barron's Educational Series, Inc.
250 Wireless Boulevard
Hauppauge, New York 11788
www.barronseduc.com

Library of Congress Control Number: 2011001278

ISBN: 978-0-7641-4578-0

Library of Congress Cataloging-in-Publication Data
Hegewald-Kawich, Horst.
[Mein Welpe. English]
    My pet series / Horst Hegewald-Kawich.
        p.   cm.
    Summary: "A care guide for care and raising of puppies, especially aimed
toward providing needed information for the early stages of dog development
and training"— Provided by publisher.
Includes bibliographical references and index.
ISBN 978-0-7641-4578-0 (pbk.)
1. Puppies.   2. Puppies—Health.   3. Puppies—Training.   I. Title.
    SF427.H44   2011
    636.7'07—dc22   2011001278

PRINTED IN CHINA
9 8 7 6 5 4 3 2 1